ISBN 978-1-330-02278-8
PIBN 10006336

1 MONTH OF
FREE
READING

at

www.ForgottenBooks.com

By purchasing this book you are
eligible for one month membership to
ForgottenBooks.com, giving you
unlimited access to our entire
collection of over 1,000,000 titles via
our web site and mobile apps.

To claim your free month visit:

www.forgottenbooks.com/free6336

English
Français
Deutsche
Italiano
Español
Português

www.forgottenbooks.com

Mythology Photography **Fiction**
Fishing Christianity **Art** Cooking
Essays Buddhism Freemasonry
Medicine **Biology** Music **Ancient
Egypt** Evolution Carpentry Physics
Dance Geology **Mathematics** Fitness
Shakespeare **Folklore** Yoga Marketing
Confidence Immortality Biographies
Poetry **Psychology** Witchcraft
Electronics Chemistry History **Law**
Accounting **Philosophy** Anthropology
Alchemy Drama Quantum Mechanics
Atheism Sexual Health **Ancient History**
Entrepreneurship Languages Sport
Paleontology Needlework Islam
Metaphysics Investment Archaeology
Parenting Statistics Criminology
Motivational

THE

HISTORY AND TRADITIONS

OF

THE ISLE OF SKYE.

BY

ALEXANDER CAMERON, Solicitor,
PROCURATOR-FISCAL AT LOCHMADDY.

INVERNESS:

E. FORSYTH, Bank Street.

1871.

INVERNESS: PRINTED AT THE ADVERTISER OFFICE, 11 BANK STREET.

PREFACE.

IT is somewhat remarkable that though nearly a century has elapsed since the writing of a history of the Isle of Skye was proposed by no less literary authority than Dr Samuel Johnson, who promised to revise the proposed work, no person has hitherto undertaken the task. This circumstance, coupled with the frequently expressed desire for such a history, and the fact that many of the interesting traditions of the island were fast passing into oblivion, induced me to devote brief intervals of leisure to collecting historical notes and traditions relating to Skye, and arranging them in the present form, which is published at the solicitation of several friends, and as a tribute to my native island. I only regret that the performance of the task I undertook, though laborious on account of the scattered and scanty sources of information, is not more worthy of the subject. It may be here stated that some of the earlier chapters of the volume were contributed by me about two years since to the columns of the *Inverness Advertiser*, and that since their publication in that newspaper they have been considerably altered and extended.

It would be tedious to enumerate all the works consulted in preparing the following pages, but those which have been made most use of are,—Tytler's History of Scotland; Gregory's History of the Western Highlands and Isles; Sir Robert Gordon's Earldom of Sutherland; Douglas's Baronage; the *Origines Parochiales Scotiæ;* the Culloden Papers; the Jacobite Memoirs; Mr Carruthers' Edition of Boswell's Tour; and Stewart's Sketches of the Highlanders.

Preface.

For much interesting and valuable information, of which I have availed myself, I am indebted to the following gentlemen:—A. K. Mackinnon, Esq. of Corry, Skye; Donald Macdonald, Esq., Tormore, Skye; Alexander Martin, Esq., banker, Portree; Sheriff Shaw of Lochmaddy; A. A. Carmichael, Esq., Lochmaddy; D. Maclachlan, Esq., S.C.D., Portree; Mr D. Nicolson, schoolmaster, Kilmuir, Skye; and Mr M. Arbuckle, schoolmaster, North Uist.

I have also gratefully to acknowledge my obligations to the Rev. A. Macgregor, M.A., of Inverness, who kindly bestowed a portion of his valuable time and attention in revising the proof sheets when the work was in the press, and whose account of the parish of Kilmuir, Skye, in the New Statistical Account of Scotland, supplied me with considerable information. My thanks are also due to Mr W. B. Forsyth, Inverness, for his attention and courtesy in making the necessary arrangements for the publication of the work.

Although my residence at a great distance from public libraries and the public records of the country, has been a disadvantage in preparing the work, I trust that but few historical facts of interest that could be ascertained have been omitted. There exist many other Skye traditions, which to limit space I omitted, but I think the most interesting are narrated.

CONTENTS.

CHAPTER V. PAGE.

CHAPTER VI.

CHAPTER VII.

CHAPTER VIII.

CORRIGENDA ET ADDENDA.

P. 37.—11th line from bottom—For 'auctionte," read 'auctorite.'

P. 44.—13th line—For '*Faiciun*,' read '*Faicinn*.'

P. 52.—11th line from bottom—For '*Eiglia*,' read '*Gigha*.'

P. 65.—24th line—For 'Dirvart,' read 'Duart.'

P. 70.—10th line from bottom—For '*Seabhar*,' read '*Leabhar*.'

P. 70.—5th line from bottom—For 'flattered,' read 'flattened.'

P. 75.—16th line—For 'thus,' read '*luchd*,' and for '*cuirn*,' read '*cuirm*.'

P. 75.—11th line from bottom—For '*An ceannadh*,' read '*A dheanadh*.'

P. 79.—11th line from bottom—For '*Aighean*,' read '*Nighean*.'

P. 83.—*Note*.—Sir Donald Macdonald's third daughter, Isabella, married Alexander Munro of Auchenbowie. She is represented now by her great-great-grandson, George Munro Binning-Home, Esquire of Argaty, who claims to be the eldest heir of line to the Earldom of Ross.

P. 84.—*Note*.—There is an error here as to the order of the marriages of Sir James Macdonald of Oransay. His first wife was Janet Macleod, and his second wife Margaret Macdonald.

P. 84.—2d line from bottom—For 'Macleed,' read 'Macleod.'

P. 113.—8th line from bottom—For 'Rushven,' read 'Rushness.'

P. 113.—4th line from bottom—For 'there,' read 'these.'

P. 150.—21st line—After 'and' insert 'gave.'

THE HISTORY AND TRADITIONS

OF

THE ISLE OF SKYE.

CHAPTER I.

THE Isle of Skye is the largest of the Western Isles, or Hebrides. It is about fifty-four miles in length, and from three to thirty-five miles in breadth, the superficial extent being about seven hundred square miles.

Skye appears at some remote period to have been exposed to violent internal convulsions, which up-heaved its steep and rugged mountains, and by breaking up the land, formed the many lochs which intersect it. The sea coast is generally high and rocky, rising into magnificent cliffs, which display the most picturesque forms, and afford a valuable index of the interior geological structure of the island. Its outline at a distance is grand and imposing, and though the landscape in the interior is for the most part bare, yet amongst its bare and rugged hills there are spots which, for wild romantic grandeur, are unsurpassed in Scotland. The general character of the surface of the island is hilly, and it is specially adapted and principally occupied for pastoral purposes, but along the coast and in some of the valleys there are fertile tracts of land, well suited for agricultural purposes, and some of which are in a good state of cultivation.

The population of Skye at the last census was 19,750, and its present annual rental is £34,917 8s 9d stg. It is divided into seven parishes, viz., — Kilmuir, Portree, Snizort, Durinish, Bracadale, Strath, and

Sleat, which embrace the smaller inhabited islands of Scalpay, Raasay, and Rona on the east coast, and Soa on the south, with several uninhabited islands, used for pasturage.

The derivation of the name of the island—Skye in English, and *Eilean Sgiathanach* in Gaelic—is somewhat obscure, but that it is so called from its winged formation (*sgiath* in Gaelic signifying wing) is most probable. There exists considerable diversity of opinion among authors on this subject, and it may be interesting to notice a few of these opinions. Dean Munro is perhaps the earliest Scotch writer that refers to the point. In his " Description of the Western Isles," through which he travelled in 1549, he writes :—" This iyle is callit by the Erishe Ellan Skyane, that is to say, in English, the Wingitt Ile, be reason it has maney wyngs and ponts lyand furth frae it, through the devyding of the loches." George Buchanan adopts the same opinion. He writes—" *Insula priscorum Scotorum sermone Skianacha hoc est, alata, vocatur quod promontorio inter quæ mare se infundit velut alæ se obtendent Usus tamen obtinuit, ut Skia id est, ala, vulgo diceretur.*" M. Martin, who was himself a native of Skye, in his " Description of the Western Isles" written in 1699, says " Skie (in the ancient language Skianach, *i.e.*, wing'd) is so called because the two opposite promontories (Vaterness lying north-west, and Troterness north-east) resemble two wings." Another learned Skyeman of the last century, Dr John Macpherson of Sleat, held a different opinion. In his " Dissertations" he writes—" When the Norwegians conquered the Western Isles, they sometimes changed the old Gaelic names of places, and gave them new ones abundantly descriptive. Thus to the Eastern Œbudæ of the ancients they gave the name of Ealand Skianach, or the Cloudy Island—Sky, in the Norse language, signifying a cloud." Pennant and Jameson are also of opinion that the name is derived from the Norwegian *Ski*, a mist. Pinkerton, while admitting the Norwegian or Gothic origin of the name, says that " Skia, corruptedly called Skye, is named from Skua, one of the Ferœ Isles." Some are of the same opinion with that expressed by James Buchanan in his "Defence of the Scots Highlanders," that the derivation is Celtic from "*skia*, a shield; *skian*, a dirk, or a sword; and *neach*, a people, *i.e., skian-neach*, these arms making up part of the dress of the inhabitants of this isle, in hostile times, when arms and war were the daily employments of these warlike people, and so might well be called *skian* and *neach*, the people with the dirks or swords." It is supposed by others that the winged temple, which Apollo had among the Hyperboreans, was situated in Skye, which from that circumstance, may have got the name of the winged isle, *Eilean Sgiathanach*. In the poems of Ossian, Skye is always called the Isle of Mist —*Eilean a Cheo*.

The earlier part of the history of Skye is so obscure, and the available sources of information so defective and conflicting, that a complete and correct sketch of its early history cannot be attempted. There has been considerable discussion among authors as to who were the first inhabitants of this country. The most probable account is that they were a colony of Celts from Gaul, a few centuries before the Christian era, who on landing in Scotland gave it its name of Alba or Albin, signifying mountainous, and who were themselves styled Albanich, but also retained their original name of Gauil or Gael. These spread themselves over the Western Isles, and would in all probability be the aboriginal inhabitants of Skye. Towards the Christian era, a colony of Goths or Scythians from Scandinavia, appear to have invaded and settled in the Western Isles, which it is said they erected into a kingdom, called *Hebudœ*, corrupted into Hebrides, in honour of their leader, Hubba. They were called *Gall*, or strangers, hence the Western Isles were also styled *Innse-gall*, Islands of the Strangers. These strangers on settling in the isles began to molest and plunder the Gael of the mainland, who very properly called the

depredators pilferers, *i.e., Piocuich,* hence Picts.   The
Picts on the other hand, despising the wandering habits
of the Gael in attending to their herds and flocks, gave
them the sobriquet *Scuits,* wanderers, hence Scots.
During the earlier centuries of the Christian era colonies
of Danes and Norwegians settled in the Western Isles.
Their presence in Skye is still manifest from the ruins
of Danish fortifications, and from the Norwegian
extraction of the names of several localities.   The
Celtic element was not, however, extinguished, either
in the population or typography of the island.

The first glimpse we have into the history of Skye—
as distinguished from general notices of the Western
Isles as a whole by some early Roman writers—is in
the Poems of Ossian, supposed to have been composed
in the early part of the third century.   He relates that
Cuthullin, son of Semo, and grandson of Cathbaid, was
about that time the chief of Skye,—Cuthullin had his
palace at Dunskaich in Sleat—a castle afterwards famous in the history of the Isles, and the gray hollow
ruins of which can still be seen.   An old Skye legend
has it, that this castle was built by Cuthullin and his
Fingalians in a single night—

> All night the witch sang, and the castle grew
> Up from the rock, with tower and turrets crowned ;
> All night she sang—when fell the morning dew
> 'Twas finished round and round—

Cuthullin had command of a numerous army, and was
renowned for his physical strength and skill in the use
of arms.   " Nor slept thy hand by thy side, chief of the
Isle of Mist ! many were the deaths of thine arm,
Cuthullin, thou son of Semo !   His sword was like the
beam of heaven when it pierces the sons of the vale ;
when the people are blasted and fall, and all the hills
are burning around."   In some of those daring attacks
by the Caledonians against the Romans it appears
Cuthullin led a party of his Skyemen.   Addressing
Fingal, King of Morven, after an unsuccessful battle
in Ireland, he says, " It is not thus thou hast seen me,

O Fingal, returning from the wars of thy lands, when the kings of the world had fled, and joy returned to the hill of hinds." Cuthullin was a great hunter, and with his hounds and favourite dog "Luath" often 'waked the thundering echoes of the rugged "Alps" of Skye —which hills still bear his mighty name. There is a long stone close to the castle of Dunskaich, to which it is said that Cuthullin's dog was tied when he was not engaged in the chase. The wisdom and valour of Cuthullin gained him such reputation in Ireland, that in the minority of Cormac, the supreme king of that country, he was chosen as guardian to the king, and General of the Irish tribes in the war carried on against Swaran, King of Lochlin, who had invaded Ireland. He left his young wife, Bragela, in his castle of Dunskaich in Skye, but she was not forgot by him, and at one of the feasts given on the eve of battle, he thus, according to Ossian, addresses the minstrels:—"O strike the harp in praise of my love, the lonely sunbeam of Dunskaich; strike the harp in praise of Bragela, she that I left in the Isle of Mist, the spouse of Semo's son! Dost thou raise thy fair face from the rock to find the sails of Cuthullin? The sea is rolling distant far, its white foam deceives thee for my sails. Retire, for it is night my love, the dark winds sigh in thy hair —retire to the halls of my feasts, think of the times that are past, for I will not return till the storm of war is ceased." Cuthullin fought with varied success in Ireland, and never returned to Skye, having been slain in battle at the early age of twenty-seven. His continued absence at the wars in Ireland was mourned with tender longing by the fair Bragela. Her sentiments on the occasion are so feelingly described by the bard, that though they lose in the translation they are well worth quoting:—"It is the white waves of the rock and not Cuthullin's sails. Often do the mists deceive me for the ship of my love! when they rise round some ghost and spread their gray skirts on the wind. Why dost thou delay thy coming, son of the generous Semo?

Four times has autumn returned with its winds, and raised the seas of Togorma, since thou hast been in the roar of battles, and Bragela distant far. Hills of the Isle of Mist! when will ye answer to his hounds? But ye are dark in your clouds. Sad Bragela calls in vain. Night comes rolling down. The face of ocean fails. The heathcock's head is beneath his wing. The hind sleeps with the hart of the desert. They shall rise with morning's light and feed by the mossy stream. But my tears return with the sun. My sighs come on with the night. When wilt thou come in thine arms, O chief of Erin's wars?" Some of the Irish bards claim Cuthullin as belonging to Ireland, and say that he merely went to Skye, for a short time, to attend the great military academy of *Domhnall*, the champion, and the Amazonian lady, *Scathach*, in order to acquire feats of arms in which he was deficient, and that Conlaoch, son of Cuthullin, was also educated in "Dunsgathach," in Skye, in all the arts of war which his father knew, with the exception of the *gathbholg*. The *gathbholg* means literally, the dart quiver. It appears to have been a fiery dart, and the same weapon which Virgil calls *cateia*, used by the Teutonic race. Cateia has been described as a compound Celtic word *gath*, or *cath*, a dart, and *tei*, of fire. Cuthullin is said to have killed his friend Ferda, by mistake, with the gathbholg, "a dart kindled into a devouring flame by the strength of wind." Fingal, or *Fionn MacChumhail*, the father of Ossian, a man of gigantic size and strength and a leader of the *Feine* or Fingalians, is said to have visited Skye on a hunting expedition about this period. The great hunt celebrated by Ossian, in which 6000 deer were killed, is commonly allowed to have been in Strath, in Skye. Fingal with his celebrated dog Bran led the chase, in which 3000 hounds were employed. There is a hill near Portree called "*Aite suidhe Fhinn,*" or Fingal's sitting place, where it is said he used to sit directing his followers at the chase, and there is a legend that a large chaldron for cooking his venison,

used to be set on three large stones near the sea shore
of Loch Snizort at Kensalyre, two of which stones are
still standing. The Lochlins or Danes began to infest the Western Isles at this time, and had frequent
sanguinary encounters with the Fingalians. A single
combat between Fingal and Manos, the King of the
Lochlins, on one of these occasions, is thus described
by the ancient bard :—

> They flung their weapons on the ground,
> And in each other grasp, the two heroes.
> When thus began the struggle of the chiefs
> It was to us a weariness to be at rest ;
> The stones and the heavy earth
> Awoke under the straining of their feet.
>   The victorious son of Cumhal lifted up
> The king of Lochlin high on his breast,
> And struck his back down to the ground
> In the midst of the ranks of Innistore.
>   Thus fell the king of Lochlin, the brave,
> In presence of all on the heath ;
> And on him, though no honour to a king,
> Was put the tie of three smalls.

The Feine or Fingalians were on the decline even in
the days of Ossian, and from the third to the eighth
century it is believed that the Lochlins or Danes were
able to make a somewhat permanent settlement in the
North Western Isles. This appears from the number
of ruins of Danish fortifications in these Isles, built
about that period. There are a great number of these
forts or *duns* in Skye ; the most conspicuous of these
are Duntulm Castle, anciently named Dun David, as
it was built and inhabited by David, one of the most
powerful of the Vikings. This castle at a later period
was the residence of the chiefs of the Macdonalds.
There are also—Dun Gherishadder, Dun Bhorve, Dun
Skerinish, Dun Skudborg, all in Troternish ; and Dun-
phaick, Dun-flo, Dun-geilb, Dun-islay, and Dun-an-
choinach, in Sleat. These forts, besides being places of
defence, served the purpose of a rude telegraph, being
built on eminences, and so placed, that each dun is in
view of some other, and by this means, when a fire was

made on a beacon in one fort, it was in a few moments after communicated to all the rest. This signal was used as an alarm at the approach of an enemy, or when suspicious vessels were seen approaching the coast.

CHAPTER II.

THE religion of Skye previous to the sixth century was Druidism. The Druids acted both as priests and judges, and were highly venerated. They were possessed of much natural wisdom and learning, which, however, was greatly marred by superstition. That their knowledge of astronomy was somewhat extensive is apparent from the manner in which their temples were built. They worshipped one God, under the name of *Beil* cr *Beathuil*, signifying the Originator of Life, in whose honour they held the festival of *Bealltainn* (May-day), on which fires were lit on each hill to welcome the rising of the sun, which they regarded as a symbol of their god *Beil*. Some superstition as to the use of fire on May-day existed at a very recent period in Skye. The Druids had also the festival of *Samhuinn* (Hallowe'en). *Samhuinn*, in Gaelic, means the fire of peace. On that evening all fires were extinguished, and it was necessary to go to the Druids for a live coal from their consecrated fires, which it was believed carried a blessing with it on the household for the whole year. A relic of this festival is still observed in the Highlands and isles, in the custom, now on the decline, of carrying lighted peats and torches on Hallowe'en. Druidism received its death-blow in the north-west of Scotland on the promulgation of Christianity by Saint Columba and his followers.

In the year 565 Columba and his twelve Christian friends left their native Erin in a *curroch*, and landed on the Island of Iona, then the stronghold of Druidism, and known as the "Isle of Druids." From thence

Columba repaired to the Court of Brudius, the King of the Picts, held at the head of Loch Ness, probably at Inverness. He was at first refused admittance, but at length succeeded, and was instrumental in altering Brudius' views so far, that he gave his consent to the gospel being preached to his subjects, and granted Columba the Island of Iona in possession. Some historians assert that it was from Conal, King of the Scots, that Columba received Iona. It is true the island was near the confines of both kingdoms, but to which it actually belonged is now difficult to ascertain. Columba was a frequent visitor and had great influence at the courts of both kings. In one of his journeys to the court of King Brudius " he remained some days in Scia or Skye, where he slew a boar." Adomnan, in his Life of Columba, mentions Skye as the scene of one of the saint's prophecies, " which was fulfilled by the arrival of an aged chief, named Artbrannan, on its shores, his reception of the truth, his baptism, his death, and his burial, all in immediate suc- cession, the last being performed *conquesto lapidum acervo,* at the mouth of a river, thence named *Tobar Artbranani.*" This aged chief received the word of God through an interpreter. Montalembert, in his Life of St Columba, gives a graphic account of this incident. He narrates that one day while Columba was labouring in his evangelical work in Skye, he cried out all at once, " My sons, to-day you will see an ancient Pictish chief, who has kept faithfully all his life the precepts of the natural law, arrive in this island; he comes to be baptised and to die." Immediately after a boat was seen to approach the shore with a feeble old man seated in the prow, who was recognised as the chief of one of the neighbouring tribes. Two of his companions took him up in their arms and brought him before the mis- sionary, to whose words, as repeated by the interpreter, he listened attentively. When the discourse was ended the old man asked to be baptised, and immediately after breathed his last breath, and was buried in the

B

very spot where he had just been brought to shore."
At Iona Columba founded Christian churches, and from
thence he and his followers went forth to the western
districts and isles of Scotland preaching the gospel.
Their efforts were signally blessed, and the dark super-
stitions of Druidism everywhere gave way to the light
of Christianity. Iona for many centuries thereafter
continued a centre of religion and learning. The mis-
sions of Columba and his followers and successors to
Skye appear to have been very successful. A great
number of places of worship were planted in the island.
Mr Donald Macqueen, minister of the parish of Kilmuir,
writing a century ago, says, " The missionaries from
Icolmkill to the Western Isles and neighbouring continent were very numerous. There are the remains of
about thirty places of worship in this and the two neighbouring parishes (Snizort and Portree), besides monas-
teries." Columba took a " special pleasure" in Skye.
He continued during all the middle ages the patron
saint of the island. There are several localities and
chapels in Skye named in honour of Columba and his
missionaries and successors. The bay of Portree was
anciently known as Saint Columba's Loch, and a small
island in the bay still bears the name of *Eilean Choluim-
cille*, Saint Columba's Island, on which he had probably
built a place of worship. A lake in the parish of Kilmuir, now drained, bore the name of Saint Columba,
and there exist traces of religious buildings, said to be
erected by him, on an island in that lake, described by
a writer of the 17th century as a " tower and a town,
and the remains of a chapel built of mortar." Pennant in 1772 writes—beneath the house of Mugastot
" was the lake of Saint Columba, now drained, once
noted for a monastery of great antiquity. The ruins
evince its age, being built with great stones, without
mortar, in the manner customary in the times of
Druidism. The cells and several rooms are still very
distinguishable. The chapel is of a later date, and
built with mortar, as are all the other chapels in Skie,

and in the little islands along its shores. These chapels were served by the monks." Martin states that there was a chapel dedicated to St Columba in the island of Troda, and also in the island of Fladda-chuan on the north coast of Skye. In the latter chapel he says the monk O'Gorgon is buried. A church dedicated to St Columba stood on an island formed by the river at the head of Loch Snizort, which in 1501 was designed as " Sanct Colmis kirk in Snesfurd, in Trouterness." The island is still used as the parish burying-ground, and it contains some very ancient tombstones. Kildonnan in Snizort is believed to have received its name from a chapel erected there to Donnan, a contemporary of Columba. Kiltaraglan (the ancient name of Portree), is said to be named from a chapel built there in memory of Talorgan, one of the Culdees. *Maol-luag,* the patron saint of Argyle, is commemorated in the chapels of Kilmoluag, in Troternish, and Kilmoluag (Clachan), in Raasay. A church dedicated to Saint Malrube stood at Kilmolruy, near Loch Eynort. There were chapels dedicated to Saint Congan in Strath, and at Glendale in Durinish. St Martin is commemorated in the chapel of Kilmartin, in Troternish, and St Clement is commemorated in *Tobar-Chlea-man,* the Well of St Clements, in Strath.

The Annals of Ulster record that the people of Skye paid tribute to Baedun, son of Cairill, king of Erin and Alban, who died in 581, and that Aidan, son of Gabran, King of Dalriada, submitted himself to him. The Scotch historians, however, assert that Aidan carried his arms into Ireland, and in several battles was so successful that he succeeded in abolishing the paying of any homage or tribute by the Scots, or inhabitants of the kingdom of Dalriada, and the inhabitants of the Western Isles, to the Kings of Ireland. The reference in the Annals to the tribute paid by the people of Skye is in Irish verse :—

Cid misi thanic a Sci,
Do ruachtus fo di sa tri
A coimed set ro clai dath
Is a duar in t Abanach.

This is translated as follows in the Chronicles of the
Picts and Scots :—

> Even I who have come from Skye,
> I have come twice and three times
> To convey gems of varying hue
> The Albanach feels neglected.

In the Annals of Tighernac and Ulster mention is
made, under the date of 668 A.D., of the voyage of the
sons of Gartnaith or Gartnaid to Ireland, with the
people of Skye.

CHAPTER III.

ABOUT the year 880 a revolution which took place in
Norway, by which Harald Harfager established himself
sole King of that country, led to a Norwegian settlement in the Western Isles. Many of Harald's oppo-
nents sought to escape his tyranny and vengeance by
leaving their native land, and settling in the Western
Isles, with the harbours of which they were well
acquainted in their former piratical cruises. Having
established themselves there, they afterwards issued to
infest and plunder the coast of Norway. Harald would
not bear their insults, and at length pursued these
pirates to their insular strongholds, and not only subdued
them, but added the whole Western Isles to the crown
of Norway, under whose dominion they continued, with
slight interruptions, for nearly four centuries. Norway
also extended its sway over the Isle of Man, whose King
was made to hold his title from that country. About
the beginning of the twelfth century, Olave the Red,
King of Man, extended his dominion over the whole
Western Isles, acknowledging the King of Norway as
his superior. His daughter, Ragnhildis, was married
in 1140 to Somerled, Prince or Lord of Argyle, from
which marriage sprung the celebrated dynasty of the
Lords of the Isles. The Chronicle of Man differs

materially from other historical accounts as to this matter, and records that "Efrica, daughter of Olaus the Swarthy, King of Man, grandfather of Harald Har-fager, was bestowed by the King of Denmark on Somerled in marriage."

Somerled is said to have been descended from an Irish race of chiefs or kings, and his descent is traced by the bards to Conn of the hundred battles *Conn-ceud-chathach*, who is said to have reigned over the half of Ireland in the second century, hence the Clan Donald Somerled's descendants adopt the patronymic "*Siol Chuinn.*" Somerled's father was named "Gillebride," and was known as *Gillebride na h-uamha* from the circumstance of his having to conceal himself in a cave in Morvern, during an invasion of the coast by the Danes. Somerled was first brought into repute by his martial skill and daring in repelling an invasion of the coast of Morvern, by Olaus (his future father-in-law) and a large army of Lochlins. At the first skirmish the clan *Aonghas Macinnis* lost their chief, and the clan adopted Somerled, who was a volunteer, tall and commanding in person, and skilful in fight, as their leader. His reputation in expelling the foreigners spread, and other tribes in Argyleshire placed themselves under his leadership. Somerled had four sons—Dougal, the ancestor of the Macdougalls of Lorn; Reginald or Ronald, from whose two sons, Donald and Ruari, were descended the Macdonalds and Macruaries respectively; Angus, who died without issue; and Gillicalane, who was slain along with his father at the battle of Renfrew, about the year 1161. In the Annals of Ulster it is stated that in the year 1208 the sons of Reginald gave battle to the men of Skye, who were slain with great slaughter (*Cath tucsat meic Raghnaill mic Somairligh, for feraidh Sciadh, du in ra marbhadh an ar*), but it does not appear that they retained possession of any part of the Island, for two years later Angus, son of Somerled, having sought to establish himself in Skye, was slain with his three sons. The Macdonalds did not obtain

a permanent footing in Skye until upwards of two centuries after this. The descendants of Somerled possessed
Argyleshire and the South Isles, while Skye and the
islands North of the Point of Ardnamurchan continued
in possession of the Kings of Man, holding under Norway.
In 1223 Paul Balkason appears as Sheriff of Skye,
under the King of Norway. He is said to be the same
person with "Pol Boke, vicecomes de Sky," who,
according to the Chronicle of Man, put out the eyes of
Godred Don at Icolmkill. The Western Isles at this
period were in a very prosperous condition. The manu-
facture of cloth and other articles was carried on to a
wonderful degree of perfection. The Hebridean chiefs,
in the exercise of piracy, then esteemed an honourable
profession, made descents upon most of the countries
on the west coast of Europe, where they plundered
castles, palaces, and churches, and carried to their
island homes silks, tapestry, jewellery, and armour. It
also is recorded that the arts, sciences, and literature
were cultivated in the Western Isles to a higher degree
than in the mainland of Scotland, or indeed in any of
the European countries. The vicinity of such enter-
prising neighbours was very irksome to the Scottish
Kings, and they made strong endeavours to get
possession of these islands. When treaty failed, they
encouraged their subjects of Scotland to invade them.
These invasions were often accompanied with circumstances of extreme cruelty. It is recorded in the
"Anecdotes of Olave the Black, King of Man," that
he went to Norway to complain to King Haco of the
great hostilities carried on by the Scotch in the Western
Isles. He was furnished in the Orkneys with a fleet
of twenty ships. "When Ottar Snackoll, Paul Bolka,
and Ungi Paul-son, heard this then sailed they south-
wards before Sky, and found in Westerford (Loch
Bracadale) Thorkel Thormodson. And they fought with
him. And Thorkel fell there and two of his sons.
But his son Thormod came off in this manner: he leapt
into a boat, which floated there by its ship, and it with

him was wrecked on Skotland." The complaints of the Islanders to the Norwegian Court of the aggressions of the Scots in the reign of Alexander III. of Scotland led to King Haco or Hacon's celebrated expedition. The Norwegian account of this expedition relates that " in summer there came letters from the Kings of the Hebrides in the western seas. They complained much of the hostilities which the Earl of Ross, Kiarnach, the son of *MacCamal,* and other Scots, committed in the Hebrides when they went to Skye. They burned villages and churches, and they killed great numbers both of men and women. They affirmed that the Scotch had even taken the small children, and raising them on the points of their spears, shook them till they fell down' to their hands, when they threw them away lifeless. They said also that the Scottish King proposed to subdue all the Hebrides if life was granted him." These tidings gave much uneasiness to King Haco, and having laid the matter before his council, it was resolved that an expedition should be sent to Scotland to revenge these injuries, and re-establish the Norwegian authority in the Isles. A large army and fleet were assembled, of which Haco took the command, and in the month of July 1263 set sail from Norway for the west coast of Scotland. Having been joined by some of his dependants in Orkney and Shetland, Haco proceeded by the Lewis to Skye, where his fleet was further augmented. The fleet now consisted of about one hundred ships, most of them large, and all well manned, and provided with arms. Haco's own ship was of great dimensions, built entirely of oak, and ornamented with richly carved dragons, overlaid with gold, reflecting the rays of the autumnal sun, and dazzling the eyes of the inhabitants of ancient Kiltaroglan (now Portree), as from the top of *Meall na h-acarsaid* they gazed on the Norwegian array of barques and galleys, as the gallant fleet proudly swept under sail through the Sound of Raasay, the north wind filling the brown sails of the noble ships and sighing through the long yellow hair of the northern marines and warriors.   The fleet anchored at the entrance to the narrow strait dividing Skye from the mainland, hence named Kyleakin *(Kyle Hacon)*, where they were joined by Magnus, King of Man, and the other petty kings of the Hebrides, with their followers.   It may be noticed that one of Haco's ships was commanded by an Andrew *Nicolson,* a surname common in Skye to this day.

From Skye the fleet proceeded to the southern islands, but Haco, not content with re-establishing his authority in the Hebrides, began to invade and ravage the neighbouring districts of Scotland, and while thus occupied at a late season of the year, his fleet suffered severely from storms, which, combined with the check received by his army at the famous battle of Largs, caused them to abandon their hostilities and steer back for the north. The shattered fleet on their return sailed by the west of Skye and called at Loch Bracadale, where Haco caused the inhabitants to supply him with provisions. From Skye the fleet retired to the Orkneys, where Haco died in December 1263—

> And they buried him in Orkney, and Norsemen never more
> Set sail to harry Scotland, or plunder on her shore.

On hearing of Haco's death, Alexander resumed his projects against the Isles, and carried on hostilities, until in the year 1265 matters were settled by a treaty made with Magnus, the successor of Haco, whereby Norway yielded to Scotland all right over the Western Isles, on payment of a sum of 4000 marks, equal to about £40,000 sterling, and a yearly quit rent of 100 marks for ever.   Since that period *Skyemen* have been *Scotchmen.*

In 1292 King John Balliol erected Skye into a Sheriffdom, which included Glenelg, Lewis, the Uists, Barra, and the Small Isles.   The lands of Skye in 1309 were granted to Hugh of Ross by King Robert Bruce. The greater part of Skye was possessed, under the Earl of Ross, by the Macleods, who were divided into two branches or clans, the *Siol Torquil,* or Macleods of Lewis, who possessed the Isle of Lewis, the districts of

Waternish, in Skye, Assynt and Gairloch, on the mainland, and the island of Raasay, where they were styled
Clann Mhic Gillechalluim ; and the *Siol Tormod* or " Macleods of Dunvegan," sometimes styled of "Harris,"
who possessed the lands of Dunvegan, Durinish,
Bracadale, Lyndale, Minginish, and Troternish in Skye,
held Harris under the Lord of the Isles, and had a
Crown grant of the lands of Glenelg,   *Torquil* and
Tormod were sons of *Leod,* who possessed the Lewis, and
from whom it is supposed to have derived its name of
Leodhas (Leod-Hus), *i.e.,* the residence of Leod.

The origin of the Macleods is traced in " Douglas's
Baronage" to Olave the Black, King of Man, a Norwegian, who in 1226, with the assistance of Paul,
Sheriff of Skye, recovered possession of the kingdom of
Man and the Isles.   Leod, the progenitor of the Macleods, was a son of Olave, by Christina, daughter of
Farquhar, Earl of Ross.   Leod, who was brought up
in the house of Paul, son of Boke, Sheriff of Skye—a
man of great power in the Isles—received from him
the lands of Harris, and from his grandfather, the Earl
of Ross, part of the barony of Glenelg.   He married
the only daughter of Macraild, a Danish knight, by
whom he received the lands of Minginish, Bracadale,
Durinish, Lyndale, Vaternish, and part of Troternish,
in Skye.   Macraild had his seat at Dunvegan Castle.
There are still families of that surname in the district
of Dunvegan or Durinish.   By the above account it
would appear that the Macleods in their origin were
connected with the founder of the Macdonald family,
Leod being the son of Olave the Black, King of Man,
and Somerled being son-in-law of Olave the Red or
Swarthy, King of Man.   This family connection was
acknowledged at an early period.   A charter of some
lands granted by Donald (grandson of Somerled),
styling himself " King of the Isles," to Lord John
Bisset, is dated at his castle of Dingwall, 19th January
1245, and witnessed by his " most beloved cousins and
counsellors" Macleod de Lewis et Macleod de Harise.

The descent of the Macleods from Olave is graphically referred to by the poetess Mary Macleod, *Mairi nighean Alastair Ruaidh,* in the *Cronan—*

> Sliochd Ollaghair nan lann,
> Thogadh srailtean ri crann,
> 'N uair a thoisich iad ann,
> Cha bu lionsgaradh gann,
> Fir a b' fhirionich baun,
> Priseil an dream
>   Rioghail gu'n chall còrach.

Some chroniclers assert that Leod was a son of a Norwegian Earl of Orkney, that he acted as vicegerent of the King of Norway over the Western Isles, and that it was his son Tormod who married Macraild of Dunvegan's daughter. The Scandinavian descent of the Macleods is referred to by Scott in his " Lord of the Isles " :—

> " Nor deem," said stout Dunvegan's knight,
> " That thou shalt brave alone the fight,
> By saints of isle and mainland both,
> By Woden wild (my grandsire's oath),
> Old Torquil will not be to lack
> With twice a thousand at his back.
> Torquil's rude thought and stubborn will
> Smack of the wild Norwegian still ;
> Nor will I barter freedom's cause
> For England's wealth or Rome's applause."

The Macleods still retain their Scandinavian names, such as—Norman *(Tormod),* Harold *(Torquil),* Olaus *(Olaghair),* and Magnus *(Manus.)* Dependent on the family of the Macleods of Dunvegan were the sept Maccrimmons. The pipers to the chiefs of Macleod were of this family. They were the most famous pipers in Scotland, and kept a training school on their farm of Borreraig, to which other Highland chiefs sent their musicians to be taught.

Contemporaneous with the Macleods were the *Clan Finnon* or Mackinnons, who possessed the district of Strath, formerly called Strathordell, from which their chiefs took their style. They are said to have been a branch of the Clan Alpine, and were at one time a very powerful family. Tighernac, the Irish historian, mentions *Cellach Macfinganne* (Mackinnon) as being, in the year 976, one of the Maormors *(Comites)* of Alba. A charter, dated 1409, by Donald, Lord of the Isles, is witnessed " Lachlan MacFingon" (Mackinnon), chief of his clan. The finest tomb in the island of Iona belongs to this family. They possessed two castles in Strath—the " Castill of Dunakyne," and the " Castill of Dunringill." The ruins of the former, known as Castle Maoil, near Kyleakin, are still conspicuous. It is said to have been built by the daughter of a Norwegian king, for the purpose of levying an impost on vessels passing through the Kyles. The Mackinnons had also an extensive estate and a residence in Mull. The chiefs of the clan "were marshals to Makoneil, Lord of the Isles, in the tym of the greatnes of that hous," and in the civil government under the Lords of the Isles it was their duty to see weights and measures adjusted. The Mackinnons were a very warlike clan, and were frequently engaged in fighting, not only for themselves, but in the cause of the neighbouring clans. The sept Macinnes acted as hereditary bowmen to the Mackinnons. Both surnames are still common in the district of Strath.

The Nicolsons though not very powerful appear to have been a very ancient family, and are said to have occupied the lands of Scorribreck in Troternish, as principal tenants since the eleventh century. A MS. History of the Macdonalds, written in the reign of Charles II., mentions " Macnicoll in Portree in Sky," as one of the sixteen men who formed the council of the Lord of the Isles. He was one of the four of the fourth rank, that is, freeholders, or men that had their lands in factory. Scorribreck House, near Portree, has been occupied by the heads of the clan or family for centuries back, until within the last fifty years. The ruins of the house attest it to have been of very great age. In 1507 King James IV. granted a letter of protection to *Mulcoill Maknicholl,* and other tenants of Troternish. The surname Nicolson is probably still the most numerous in the district of Troternish.

CHAPTER IV.

THE islanders afforded material assistance to Robert
the Bruce in rescuing the crown of Scotland from the
English. He had the support of the Lord of the Isles,
and of all the west coast chiefs, with the exception of
his inveterate enemy, the Macdougall of Lc
Earl of Ross acknowledged Bruce, and j
standard; and we may be assured that his
Skye fought at the glorious battle of Banı
The mustering of the Skyemen on that occasic
graphically described by Scott:—

> 'Twas then that warlike signals wake
> Dunscaith's dark towers, and Eisord's lake,
> And soon from Caligarrigh's head
> Thick wreaths of eddying smoke were spread.
> A summons these of war and wrath
> To the brave clans of Sleat and Strath;
> And ready at the sight,
> Each warrior to his weapon sprung,
> And targe upon his shoulder flung
> Impatient for the fight.
> Mackinnon's chief in warlike gray
> Had charge to muster their array,
> And guide their barks to Brodick Bay.

Tormod Macleod was the chief of Dunvegaı
reign of King Robert Bruce. He was succeedı
son Malcolm, who left three sons—John, h
Tormod, progenitor of some families of the
Macleod in Harris; and Murdo, ancestor of t   ___cle-
leods of Gesto. About the year 1343 King David II.
granted to the above named Malcolm, chief of Macleod,
" Two-thirds of the tenement of Glenelg, namely,
eight darachs and five pennylands, for the service of a
ship of twenty-six oars when required." Malcolm
Macleod was succeeded in the chieftainship by his son
John. Nothing remarkable is related of him. He had
two sons, Malcolm, the eldest, who predeceased him,
and William, his heir, who was at first designed for

the Church, and was surnamed William *Clerach* (the clerk.)   William, however, distinguished himself more as a warrior than as a man of peace.   He made a raid upon that part of Lovat's lands called Aird, in revenge of an injury he received in his youth.   He brought the cattle seized by his men to Skye, and slaughtered them in Harlosh.   He was also at variance with some branch of the Macdonalds.   A daughter of John Maclean of Lochbuy was married to William, by whom he had three sons—John, who succeeded him in the chieftainship; Tormod, of whom are descended the family of Macleods having the patronymic *Mac Mhic Uilleim,* and George, who went abroad and settled in Lorraine, of whom there are several families there.   John Macleod of Dunvegan accompanied the Lord of the Isles to the battle of Harlaw, in 1411.   He was married to a daughter of Douglas, by whom he had two sons—William, the heir ; and Tormod, ancestor of the Macleods of Drynoch and Balmeanach ; and one daughter, Margaret, who was married to Roderick Macleod of Lewis. John Macleod died in Harris, and was succeeded by his son William, who afterwards proved his valour in arms, and commanded his clan for many years, until slain in battle at an advanced age.

In 1335 Edward Balliol conferred the Island of Skye on John of the Isles for his allegiance, and in the following year the grant was confirmed by Edward III. That grant was superseded by King David II., who granted Skye anew to the Earl of Ross.   In 1369 King David II. came so far north as Inverness, to suppress a rebellion of John of the Isles.   John made his submission to him then, and gave hostages for his future conduct.   The hostages from Skye were allowed *one penny and a halfpenny* a day for their expense, while those from Caithness were only allowed *one penny.*   In the following year William, Earl of Ross, resigned the lordship of Skye which King David II. granted anew to him, " with remainder, to Sir Walter of Lesley and Eufame, his wife, and their heirs male, or in deficiency of heirs male, to the eldest daughter of Eufame herself, and of her female heirs." " About the year 1382, Eufame, Countess of Ross, resigned the barony and lordship of Skye, which King Robert II. then granted to his son, Alexander Stewart, Earl of Buchan, and to the same Eufame." The lands of Sleat, in Skye, were held by Godfrey, the son of John, Lord of the Isles, between the years 1389 and 1401, but the descendants of " mighty Somerled," or Macdonalds, did not become permanently settled in Skye until the middle of the fifteenth century. The circumstances which led to their position there are as follows :—Donald, Lord of the Isles (whose mother was a daughter of King Robert II.), having married Mary Lesley, only daughter of the Earl of Ross, succeeded to the Earldom in 1411, after a sharp contest with the Regent, Duke of Albany, who opposed his claims, in the course of which was fought the sanguinary battle of Harlaw, commemorated both in Scotch and Celtic song. In this manner Skye came into the hands of the Lord of the Isles. In the year 1449, Alexander, Earl of Ross, and Lord of the Isles, who was married to a daughter of the Earl of Huntly, died at his castle of Dingwall, leaving three sons—John, Earl of Ross and Lord of the Isles, Celestine, Lord of Lochalsh, and Hugh, Lord of Sleat in Skye. Hugh took up his residence in the ancient castle of Dunscaich, in Sleat. In addition to the district of Sleat, Hugh was nominal proprietor under his brother, Earl John, of lands in Uist, Benbecula, and the mainland, in the possession of which he was opposed by his relations the Clan Ranald of Garmoran. The charter by John, Earl of Ross and Lord of the Isles, by which, with consent of his council, he granted to his brother " Hugh Macalester of Isles, Lord of Slete, and to his heirs male, legitimate or illegitimate, by Fynvola Macalester Mac-Ian of Ardnamurchan, and their lawful heirs, with remainder to Hugh's heirs male, by any other wife chosen after the death of Fynvola, with advice of John of Yle, and his kinsmen, &c.," 28 marklands of Slete,

60 marklands in the north part of Uist, 30 marklands of Skerehong in South Uist, and 12 marklands of Beanbeacla, is dated at Aros 1449, and is witnessed by William Macleod of Dunvegan. In 1495 King James IV. confirmed this grant at Stirling. "Huchone of the Iles of Slet," is mentioned as one of the council of John, Earl of Ross and Lord of the Isles, in an indenture between Hector Maclaine of Lochbuy and John Ross of Balnagown, dated at Dingwall in the year 1475. Hugh of Sleat was a powerful warrior, and was not only able to maintain his rights, but ravaged the Orkney Islands in company with William Macleod of Dunvegan and Harris, and other island chiefs in the year 1460. Hugh died about the year 1495, and was succeeded by his son John. The descendants of Hugh increased very rapidly in the following century, and became of much repute. They were known as the *Clann Uisdean,* to distinguish them from the other branches of the Macdonalds.

John, Lord of the Isles, having been rather liberal in granting lands to the Macleods, Macleans, and Macneils, his son Angus (who was married to a daughter of the Earl of Argyle), rose in rebellion against him. Angus was assisted by the several branches of the Macdonalds, while the other clans assisted the father. The contest was ended by a great sea-fight, which took place in a bay in the Island of Mull in the year 1480. This engagement is known as " the battle of the bloody bay." William Macleod of Dunvegan was slain there. In 1493 John, Lord of the Isles, was forfeited and deprived of his titles and estates. Several rebellious attempts having been made by the island chiefs to restore the forfeited title, James IV. was induced to make excursions to the west coast to quell these insurrections and bring the chiefs to submission. On one of these occasions, John of Sleat, Hugh's son, made his submission to the King at Mingarry Castle, in Ardnamurchan, in the month of May 1495. In 1505 John of Sleat resigned into the hands of King James

IV. the lands of Sleat and Uist held by him, and they were granted by the King to " Ranald Alansonn of Yland Bagrin," South Uist, the chief of Clanranald. John who had no family of his own, appears to have divested himself of his estates from selfish motives, and from a dislike to his other brothers, who were not full brothers, Hugh, their father, being married more than once.   The *Clann Uisdean* were thus, on the death of John, which took place shortly after his resignation, left without legal rights to any property in Skye, or in any of the other Isles, so that for some time they held their lands in Skye and North Uist without any title.

John of Sleat having died without issue, was succeeded by Donald Gallach, his brother, a son of Hugh by his second wife, a lady of the Clan Gunn, and daughter of the Crowner or Sheriff of Caithness.   Donald was called *Gallach,* from the circumstance of his having been fostered in Caithness by his mother's relations. He took possession of the lands of Sleat, and the castle of Dunskaich, where he resided.   He had a brother, also called Donald, whose mother was a daughter of the Laird of Macleod, and who was known by the name of *Donald Herrach,* from his having been born in Harris. The two brothers were cruelly murdered by their natural or rather *unnatural* brother, Gilleasbuig Dubh (Archibald the Black), an ambitious and turbulent man, who sought by these cruel and tragic means to seize upon the property of his brothers and become chief of the clan, in which he was for a time successful.   This happened about the year 1506.   The following is the traditional account of these cruel assassinations :—

Donald Herrach resided in North Uist, which estate he held under his brother Donald Gallach ; he was not only possessed of influence and power, but was famed for his personal bravery and strength.   Gilleasbuig Dubh had therefore to resort to strategy before he could overpower him.   He along with some other associates went to pay Donald an ostensibly friendly visit, and after enjoying his hospitality, they proposed to have some gymnastic exercises, such as who should leap highest, at which they knew Donald was most expert. They had previously contrived that an accomplice named Paul should place a thong with a running noose over the place where the leap was to be taken, and through the wooden partition of the apartment in which they were met, while he remained concealed on the opposite side, ready when Donald Herrach leaped to get the noose round his neck and strangle him, while the rest of the assassins could with more safety to themselves finish him. This they did by running a red-hot spit through his body. Gilleasbuig got the lands of North Uist for the time, and also possession of Donald Herrach's eldest son Ranald; the other son Angus *Fionn* having been removed by his nurse to Skye, where on coming to age he obtained some lands in Troternish, and afterwards when on a visit to Uist revenged his father's death by shooting an arrow at the infamous Paul, which pierced him in the heel, as he was crossing a rivulet that bounded the sanctuary of Kilmuir, to which place he was making his escape.

After having disposed of Donald Hearrach, Gilleasbuig went to Skye to visit his brother, Donald Gallach of Sleat, who received him kindly. They went where a galley was building for Donald, and he having requested Gilleasbuig's opinion of her, Gilleasbuig observed that there was something deficient under the bow. On Donald's stooping down to examine it, Gilleasbuig drew his dirk and stabbed him to the heart. He took possession of the Macdonald estates in Skye and Uist, and singular enough, not only preserved the lives of the eldest sons of both his brothers, but performed all the duties of a guardian towards them. His inhuman conduct to his brothers roused some of their relations, and he was expelled from North Uist, where he resided, by Ranald Allanson of Moydert, and took for some time to piracy. He afterwards returned to Skye, and being a man of ability, seized command of the clan, and assumed the office of Bailie of Troternish, hitherto held by Mac-

leod of Dunvegan. His right, by whatever means
obtained, was recognised by the Government in 1510,
and a letter in his favour was directed under the Privy
Seal to the tenants of Troternish, in which they were
ordered not to disturb him, his factors or his servants
in their persons, their goods, or their peaceable possession of the leases which Gilleasbuig had from the King
in Troternish, and especially in his execution of the
office of Bailie.

Gilleasbuig's sway was but short-lived, for he soon
met the fate he deserved, having, when engaged in a
deer hunt in North Uist, been slain by his nephews,
Donald *Gruamach*, or Grimlooking, son of Donald
Gallach, and Ranald, son of Donald Herrach. Donald
Gruamach determining to have a quarrel with his unnatural uncle, let slip his own hound at the first stag
they met, which offended Gilleasbuig and caused him
to reprimand him ; Donald retorting, said that he had
a much better right to do so than he had, at the same
time giving his uncle a blow. Gilleasbuig upon this
called Ranald, told him that Donald had struck him,
and asked for his sword, which Ranald carried for him.
Donald said, " Give it to him, Ranald, and remember
your father's death, and my father's." Upon which
Ranald drew the sword and slew Gilleasbuig on the spot.
This took place in the glen between the hills of North
and South Lee, near Lochmaddy, since called *Bealach a
Sgaill*. On the return of the nephews to Gilleasbuig's
residence, his wife asked them if they had good sport
that day. One of them answered, " We killed the
tallest stag in the forest." She at once conjectured
that her husband had been slain, and gave apt expression
to her grief in the following Gaelic couplet, still preserved in the oral traditions of Uist :—

Is truagh nach mise bha sa ghleann,
Far an d'rinneadh feoil 's far an do dhoirteadh fuil,
Far an do leagadh an damh duilleach donn,
Mo chreach lom ! nach robh mi muigh.

William Macleod of Dunvegan, on his death at the

battle of Bloody-bay, was succeeded by his son Alexander, commonly known as the Humpbacked, or *Alastair Crottach.* He was a chief of great activity, both in peace and war. He built one of the towers of Dunvegan Castle, and repaired the church or monastery of Saint Clement's, in Rodil, Harris. In the month of August 1498 he made his submission to King James IV., at the royal Castle of Campbelton, in Kintyre, when the King granted in heritage to him " two unciate of the lands of Trouternes, together with the bailiary of the whole lands of Trouternes, lying in Skye in the Lordship of the Isles, for service of ward, relief, and marriage, with the maintenance of a ship of 26 oars, and two ships of 16 oars, both in peace and war for the use of the King, or his lieutenants, reserving to the King the nests of falcons within the lands, and all other usual services. In October of the same year the King granted to Torquil Macleod of Lewis, and to his heirs by Catherine Campbell, sister of Archibald, Earl of Argyle, the office of bailie of the lands of Troternish, and four marks of the *terunga* of Duntullyn (Duntuilm), and four marks of Ardvetfullan (Ardmhiceolan), which belonged to that office, all which had been forfeited by John, Lord of the Isles." Both these Charters were shortly thereafter revoked by the king. Alexander Macleod of Dunvegan was married to a daughter of Allan Cameron of Lochiel, by whom he had three sons —William, Donald, and Tormod (who successively became chiefs of the clan)—and a daughter who was married to James Macdonald (son of Donald Gruamach of Sleat), who possessed Castle Camus, in Sleat. On the death of James she was married to Allan MacIan Muydertach, captain of Clanranald, who built the castle of Ormiclate, and the church of Howmore, in South Uist, both now in ruins. This Allan was father of Sir Donald Macdonald of Clanranald, a distinguished warrior.

The notorious massacre of the Macdonalds of Eig occurred during the chieftainship of Alexander Macleod of Dunvegan. It does not, however, appear to have been noticed by any historian of the period, the sad tale being merely preserved in the oral traditions of Skye and Eig. It is related that a boat, manned by three young men of the Macleods, while on their way from Mull to Dunvegan, landed at Eig. The Macleods having shown some disrespect towards some Eig young women, were seized by the Eigites, bound hand and foot, and placed in their own boat, which, being towed out to sea was set adrift. The wind and current being favourable, the boat drifted towards the entrance of Dunvegan Loch, where it was picked up by the chief of Macleod, who was returning in his large galley from Orkney. His helpless clansmen were conveyed to Dunvegan Castle, and their wants attended to, while the enraged chief assembled a number of his warriors and sailed for Eig, determined to revenge the ill treatment of his clansmen. The people of Eig on espying the galleys of the Macleods approaching the island, feared the vengeance of the Macleods, and betook themselves to a large cave in the south of the island, where they concealed themselves for some time. Unfortunately, however, one of their number ventured out to spy the movements of the invaders, who after a fruitless search had gone on board their galleys, and were about leaving the harbour. He was observed by the Macleods, who immediately landed and traced his footsteps to the cave. The Macdonalds refused to surrender, thinking themselves safe, as from the narrow entrance to the cave they could easily prevent any of the Macleods from entering. Macleod then caused a large fire of turf and ferns to be kindled at the entrance of the cave, the smoke of which suffocated all within :—

> The warrior threat, the infant's plain,
> The mother's screams were heard in vain ;
> The vengeful chief maintains his fires,
> Till in the vault a tribe expires !
> The bones that strew that cavern's gloom
> Too well attest their dismal doom.

The affair at Trumpan is said to have taken place before the massacre in Eig, but there are no means of fixing the date. It appears a feud existed between the Macleods of Waternish, who were of the Siol Torquil, and the Macdonalds of Uist. The Macleods were assembled on a Sunday in the church of Trumpan, Waternish, when the Macdonalds coming suddenly upon them, set the building on fire, and all the worshippers were burned, with the exception of one woman, who in the confusion escaped by a window. The flame and smoke—the usual telegraph of those days—soon warned the inhabitants of the neighbouring districts, who made for the scene, and before the Macdonalds could regain their boats, which by the receding of the tide, were high and dry upon the rocks at Ardmore, they were attacked by the Macleods. A desperate struggle ensued, in which all the Macdonalds were slain. Their bodies were ranged in line alongside a turf dyke, near the scene of the fight, and the dyke was tumbled over on the top of them—a quick but unfeeling form of burial. This fight is known as *Blar milleadh garaidh, i.e.,* the battle of the spoiling of the dyke.

King James IV. did much to promote peace and order in the Western Isles, and not only succeeded in suppressing various feuds among the islanders and in establishing his authority, but gained the confidence of the islanders so much, that many of them joined his standard and accompanied him to the field of Flodden. He was not only content to maintain the royal authority by force of arms, but endeavoured to promote religion and the knowledge of the laws of Scotland in the isles. In 1501 he presented Sir Archibald Berchame, chaplain to the parsonage of " Sanct Colmis Kirk in Snesfurd" (Snizort), with the " annexis and vicarages" of the same, namely—*Kilmolowock in Rasay* and *Kilmory in Watternes.* To the rectory and vicarage of *Kilcrist* in the parish of Strath, he in 1505, presented Sir Kenneth Adamsoun, chaplain, in room of the deceased Sir John Johne Makgillebridesoun. Three years later John Ranaldsoun was presented to be clerk to the

rectory of the said church.   In 1511 the king presented
Master John Monro to the rectory of *Mygnes* in Bracadale.   In the following year he presented Sir Donald
Rede to the rectory of " Uig in Trouternes," vacant by the
demission of Sir Nicolas Brachan.   In 1508 he granted,
during his pleasure, to Kaneth Willyamsoun the
Crown lands of the *terunga* of Kilmartin, and half of
the *terunga* of Baronesmor in Trouternes of the old
extent of six marks, to support the said Kaneth at the
schools " for to lere and study the Kingis lawis of
Scotland and afterwart to exers and vse the sammyn
within the boundis of the Ilis."   In the same year the
King gave a commission to Andrew, Bishop of Caithness, Ranald Allansoun of Ylan-bigern (Island Begrum
Castle, South Uist), and Alexander Macleod of Dunvegan, to let to sufficient tenants for five years, the
lands of the Lewis and Waternish in Skye, forfeited by
Torquil Macleod of the Lewis.

CHAPTER V.

IMMEDIATELY after the death of the King at Flodden
in 1513, and during the minority of Donald Gruamach
of Sleat, an attempt was made, headed by Alexander
Macleod of Dunvegan, and Lachlan Maclean of Duart,
to restore the Lordship of the Isles in the person of
Sir Donald of Lochalsh, who was knighted on the field
of Flodden.   They seized the royal Castle of Carne-
burgh in Mull, and Macdonald's Castle of Dunskaich
in Sleat, and threatened with fire and sword all who
resisted the authority of the new Lord of the Isles.
The rebellion was joined by several chiefs, and John,
Duke of Albany, not being able wholly to suppress it,
was obliged to treat with the rebels.   He granted to
Macleod and Maclean, and their servants, landed men,
gentlemen, and yeomen, a remission, to last from 6th
September 1515 to 1st January 1516, for all past

crimes, and in particular for besieging and taking the said castles and holding them against the Regent, and for assisting Sir Donald Ilis of Lochalch, and his accomplices. About this time Castle Camus, in Sleat, was besieged by the Macleods for a long time. The siege was raised by the intrepidity of a lady, styled Mary of the Castle. Alexander Macleod of Dunvegan had a safe conduct from the Regent, under the privy seal of King James V., to pass to any place within Scotland from 6th January to 15th March 1517. On 12th March of the same year Macleod made his submission to King James V., his Regent and Council, when he and his friends received a remission for assisting Sir Donald Ilis of Lochalch, when he took part with Lord Hume in his treasonable proceedings. Macleod at this time asked for an heritable grant of the lands of Troternish, on account of holding an old title to them, but which was not recognised by the Government. He was refused a grant of the lands, but was continued King's tenant for eleven years, and thereafter during the will of the Regent.

Donald Gruamach of Sleat did much to raise- the power of the Macdonalds of Skye, or *Clann Uisdein.* He was also styled Donald *Isles* of Sleat, and from him the heads of the family had their patronymic of *Mac-Dhomhnuill nan Eilean,* or Macdonald of the Isles. In his martial undertakings he received considerable assistance from the *Siol Torquil,* on account of his mother having been first married to Torquil Macleod of the Lewis, chief of the *Siol Torquil.* In 1524 he entered into a bond of friendship with the chief of the Clan Mackintosh. About the year 1528 Donald Gruamach and his clan, with the help of his uterine brother John Mactorquil Macleod of the Lewis, and his followers, succeeded in expelling Macleod of Dunvegan and those of his clan that were settled in the district of Troternish. The Macdonalds then took possession of and occupied the district. In acknowledgment of his services, Donald Gruamach assisted John Mactorquil

Macleod in recovering the Lewis from Malcolm Macleod, his uncle, who had, on the forfeiture of Torquil, John's father, assumed command of the clan, and taken possession of the Lewis—of which he procured a royal grant.   John Mactorquil retained possession of the Lewis without a title for a number of years.   About the year 1529 Alexander (MacIan Cathanach), chief of the Macdonalds of Islay, and several of the island chiefs, were in rebellion on account of an Act of the Privy Council, declaring the grants of Crown lands in the Isles by the Earl of Angus to be null.   The Earl of Argyle sought to enforce this Act, and a series of ravages was the consequence.   The Council ordered the tenants of the Isles to be summoned to appear before the King on the 24th May 1530 " to commune with His Majesty for good rule of the Isles."   Sometime in course of that month Donald Gruamach of Sleat, Alexander Macleod of Dunvegan, and seven other of the principal island chiefs, sent an offer of submission to the King, who granted them a protection against the Earl of Argyle, provided they came to Edinburgh, or wherever the King held his court for the time, before the 20th June, and remain as long as the King required their attendance, it being understood that the protection was to last for twenty days after their departure home.   In the following year Donald Gruamach of Sleat, Alexander Macleod of Dunvegan, and Ewen Mackinnon of Strathardill were frequently cited before Parliament, but failed to appear.

Ranald Macdonald Herrach, cousin of Donald Gruamach, and his associate, when Gilleasbuig Dubh was slain, went after that event to Ireland, where he is said to have distinguished himself as a warrior and leader, under the Antrim family.   Having been severely wounded in battle, he returned to Skye, accompanied by a medical attendant named Maclean, whose descendants were settled at Cuidrach in Skye, and of whom was the late Sir Lachlan Maclean of Sudbury. Ranald afterwards resided at Griminish, in North Uist, and from him are descended the family of Macdonalds of Balranald in that island. He occasionally crossed from North Uist to Sleat to visit his cousin at the Castle of Dunskaich. On one of these occasions it is said that he was disgusted to find twelve of the Macdonalds of Clanranald revelling without control at Dunskaich, presuming on the protection of Donald Gruamach's lady, who was a daughter of Clanranald. Despising the good nature of his cousin in permitting such liberties in his castle, Ranald seized upon the twelve revellers early of a morning and hung them up to a part of the walls of the castle fronting their kinswoman's bedroom window. He immediately went to his cousin and told him he was setting off for Uist. Donald pressed him to remain with them for some time longer, and in no event to leave until his wife had some breakfast prepared. Ranald declined, and replied that he was sure the sight she would behold on looking out from her window, would not incline her to thank him for his morning's work. He immediately left the castle and set sail for North Uist. It is supposed that this transaction led Donald Gruamach's lady to instigate Mackinnon, their steward, to assassinate Ranald, which he did a few years after this event at a place marked by a cairn in Balmore of North Uist.

Donald Gruamach died in 1537, and was succeeded in the chieftainship by his son Donald Gorme Macdonald. Donald Gorme married the heiress of John Mactorquil Macleod of the Lewis. Alexander Macleod of Dunvegan and his clan contrived to resume possession of the disputed district of Troternish. Donald Gorme procured the assistance of Siol Torquil of Lewis, and in May 1539, the combined forces of the Siol Torquil and Macdonalds invaded and laid waste Troternish, expelling the Macleods at the point of the sword. Tradition relates that the allies followed the Siol Tormod to Skeabost, where a battle was fought at a place called *Achnafala* (the field of blood), and that several heads that had been cut off in the fray floated by the river

E

Snizort into the yair at the mouth of the river, hence still called *coire-nan-ceann*, the yair of heads. The family residence of the chiefs of the Macdonalds was shortly thereafter transferred from the ancient Castle of Dunskaich, to the strong and commodious Castle of Duntulm, in Troternish.

After his success in Troternish, Donald Gorme attempted to assume the forfeited title of Lord of the Isles and Earl of Ross. Sir John Mackenzie of Kintail and his clan were opposed to his pretensions, and determining to revenge himself on them, Donald Gorme with a large party invaded and ravaged the districts of Kinlochew and Kintail. Many of the Mackenzies were slain, among whom were Sir Dugald Mackenzie, priest of Kintail, who resided at Glenshiel. Taking advantage of the absence of Sir John, and hearing that his strong Castle of Elandonnan was slightly guarded, Donald Gorme attempted to take the castle by surprise. While so engaged, he received a wound from an arrow in the thigh, which proved fatal. The arrow was aimed at him by Duncan Macrae, a warrior who had come to the assistance of the keepers of the castle. It was his last arrow, and the Macdonalds were in the act of breaking the iron gate of the castle when this untoward event caused them to desist. Donald Gorme, in hastily pulling the barbed arrow out of the wound, severed an artery, and no means could be devised to check the effusion of blood. He was conveyed by his men to a small islet out of reach of the castle, where a hut was hastily constructed, in which, in a very short time he expired. The islet still receives the name of the site of Macdonald's house, *Larach-tigh-Mhic-Dhonuill*. The Macdonalds, discouraged by the death of their chief, returned to Skye, having first burned all the boats they could find in Kintail. On 22d March 1541, King James V. granted a remission to Archibald Ilis, *alias* Archibald the Clerk, and Alexander, both sons of Donald Gallach of Sleat, and various others, for their "treasonable burning of the Castle of Allanedonnand,

and of the boats there, and the hereschip of Kinlochow and Trouternes." Donald Gorme left a young son also named Donald, who afterwards became chief of the clan. During his minority his granduncle and guardian, Archibald Ilis or the Clerk, acted for some years as captain of the clan.

CHAPTER VI.

KING JAMES V., with a determination to suppress the existing feuds, and to prevent in future such rebellious schemes as that of Donald Gorme's assumption of the lordship of the isles, resolved to appear in person in the Western Isles with a fleet. Preparations for the voyage were accordingly made on a grand scale. On the 22d May 1540, the royal fleet sailed from the Forth. The king and the many barons, gentlemen, and soldiers in his train, appropriated six of the ships of war. Three ships were occupied separately by Cardinal Beaton, the Earl of Huntly, and the Earl of Arran each with a force of 500 soldiers, besides officers; and the remaining three ships carried the provisions and military stores. Having doubled Cape Wrath, the fleet steered for the Lewis, Harris, and Uist, and crossed to Loch Dunvegan, in Skye, where Alexander Macleod, the chief, and other leading men of his clan, were seized and taken on board. From Dunvegan the fleet coasted round by the north of Skye, touching at Duntulm, where the king inspected and expressed his admiration of the fortifications of the castle, and arriving at the harbour of Portree, then called *Loch Choluim-cille*, the ships dropped anchor. Tradition bears that the army landed on the rock upon which the present Scorribreck House is built, hence called *Creag-na-mor-shluagh*, the rock of the multitude; and that the king and his suit landed at a small creek farther east, hence called *Port-an-Righ*, the king's landing place, which thereafter became the name of the loch and parish. Hugh Miller described the entrance to Portree Loch as " singularly majestic— the cliffs tower high on either side in graceful magnificence . . . . a palace gateway erected in front of some homely suburb that occupies the place which the palace itself should have occupied." On this occasion the interior was more in keeping with the ' palace gateway.' The hills enclosing the harbour were covered with trees, while a forest of bright masts rigged in briliant colours filled the bay, and amid the camp pitched on the rising ground, upon which the town of Portree is now erected, flags and banners fluttered in the breeze, while the spacious snow-white pavilion of the king displayed numerous glittering bannerets, above which waved the royal standard. While in this district of Skye the king was waited upon by John Moydertach, captain of Clanranald, Alexander of Glengarry, and other cheftains of the Macdonalds, who probably hoped, by their submission, to secure the royal pardon and favour before the King visited their own districts. On leaving Portree and giving it a royal name, though not a royal charter, the King proceeded south, landing at Kintail, Glenelg, and other places along the coast, until he arrived at Dumbarton. As the fleet swept along, the natives flocked to the shore to gaze on the unusual sight, and the island chiefs crowded round the royal pavilion, generally pitched upon the beach, " to deprecate resentment, and proffer allegiance." Lesley, Bishop of Ross, in his history of this period gives the following account of this expedition :—" Eftir that the King had pacyfiet his haill bourdouris, and all the partis of his realme, throuch the exerceing justice, and traivelling be himself in propper persoun in all placeis to that effect, as neid requyrit sua that thair wes als gret quietnes, tranquilitie and pollitie in Scotland as evir wes in ony Kingis tyme of befoir ; yit nochttheles thair wes some in the Ilis quha wald not cum to obedience ; quhairfir the King causit prepare any navy of guid schippis, and past himself thairintill, being accumpanyit be the Erlis of Arrane, Huntley, Argyll, and mony utheris erlis, lordis, baronis; and scippit in the raid of Leithe in the moneth of May, and salit be the coastis of Fyff, Angus, Aberdene, by Murray firthe, Suthirland, and Caithnies, quhill he come to Orknay; quhair he landit and all his company, and wer honorablie ressavit be the Bischop thairof, callit Robert Maxwell, and thair renewit thair victuallis as wes necessar with freishe meitts; and thairfra salit to the Isles of Sky and Lewis, quhair M'Clewde of the Lewis, and the principallis of his kin, war brocht unto the King; sic lyk, send ane cumpanye to M'Clewde, Hariche, quha come furth of his Ile to the Kingis presens alsua. And thaireftir salit be the coast of Ros, by Kintaill, to the Ile of Trauternes quhair diverse of M'Coneylli's kin, sic as the laird of Glengarry, Johne Moydert, and utheris, quha allegeit thame to be of the principalle bluide, and lordis of the Iles wes brocht lykewayis to the Kingis presens. And thairfra cummand to Kintire, Knapdane, and the rest of the Ilis, Maclane and James M'Oneile beand the tua principall capitanes of the small ilis, come to the King sic lyk; and the King himself landit at Dumbartane, and send the capitanes and schippis with the presoneris theivin about the Ilis; the same way thay come to Edinburgh, and eftir that landing thair, the principallis of thame wes keipit in warde as plegis fir guide reule of the cuntrey, quhair they remanit during the Kingis tyme; quhilk wes the caus that thair wes also greit quietnes and obedience to the auctionte in all the Ilis as thair wes in ony uther part of the realme, and also gude compt and payment maid yeirly to the Kingis comptroller in his eschekker fir the landis of the Ilis parteyning to the crown as for any uther part of the patrimony on the mayne land."

King James V. died in 1542, upon which the Highlands and Isles were again in disorder, and the island chiefs took arms in support of the claims of Donald Dubh, to the forfeited Lordship of the Isles. Donald was son of Angus, son of John, last Lord of the Isles.

Among his Barons and Council were Alexander Macleod of Dunvegan ; Archibald Macdonald, captain of the Clan-uisdean, or Macdonalds of Sleat (the chief, Donald, son of Donald Gorme, being then a minor) ; and Ewin Mackinnon of Strathardill. Donald Dubh, and his Island followers, joined the Earl of Lennox in the interest of England : and in the summer of 1545 they went to Ireland, and having taken the oath of allegiance to the King of England, joined the English army there. In the despatches sent from the Irish Privy Council to Henry VIII., Donald Dubh's army of 4000 are described as "three thousand of them very tall men, clothed, for the most part, in habergeons of mail, armed with long swords and long bows, but with few guns ; the other thousand tall maryners that rowed in the galleys." Donald Dubh died of fever in Ireland, and was buried at the expense of the King of England, with great pomp. His followers dispersed.

In 1547 Alexander Macleod of Dunvegan died at an advanced age, and was buried within the church of St Clements, at Rodil, Harris. His tomb is still in good preservation. It is finely sculptured with some interesting devices, and bears a Latin inscription, and several mottoes. He was succeeded in the chieftainship and estates by his son William, who was married to Agnes Fraser, daughter of Hugh, fourth Lord Lovat, by whom he had an only daughter, Mary—afterwards married to Duncan Campbell, younger of Auchinbreck.

CHAPTER VII.

Donald Munro, High Dean of the Isles, travelled through most of the Western Isles in 1549, of which he has given an interesting description. In describing "the grate Ile of Sky" he writes, "In this Ile there is 12 paroche kirkes manurit and inhabit, fertill land namelie for aites, excelling aney uther ground for grassing and pastoures . . . maney woods, maney forests, maney deire, fair hunting games, maney grate hills, &c. Within this iyle of Sky there is 5 castills, to wit, the castill of Dunbeggan, perteining to M'Cloyd of Herray, ane starke strengthe, biggit upon ane craig; the castill of Dunakyne, perteining to Mackynnoun; the castill of Dunringill, perteining to the said Mackynnoun; the castill of Camus in Sleit, perteining to Donald Gormeson; the castill of Dunskay, perteining to the said Donald Gormeson; and the castill of Doun-twylme, perteining to Donald Gormeson likeways." Of the small island of Pabay belonging to Mackinnon, he writes that it " is full of woodes, guid for fishing, and a main shelter for thieves and cut-throats." There is not a tree now on the island, and only one family—a shepherd's—is resident there; the " thieves and cut-throats" have vanished like the fairies. He speaks of the island of Raasay of which, and of the Parish of " Sneisport" (Snizort), he is believed to have been at one time vicar, as having " twa castles, to wit, the castle of Kilmorocht, and the castle of Brolokit, with twa fair orchards at the saids twa castles, with ane paroche kirk callit Killmolowocke, ane rough countrey, but all full of freestanes and guid quarelles. It is excellent for fishing, perteining to M'Gillychallan of Raarsay, be the sword, and to the bishope of the iles be heritage. This same M'Gillychallan should obey M'Cloyd of the Lewis. At the north end of Raarsay be half myle of sea frae it layes ane ile callit Ronay, maire than a myle in lengthe, full of wood and heddir, with ane havein for heiland galeys in the middle of it, and the same havein is guid for fostering of thieves, ruggairs, and reivairs, till a nail, upon the peilling, and spulzeing of poor pepill. This ile perteins to M'Gillychallan of Raarsay by foree, and to the bishope of the iles be heritage." Raasay and Rona appear to have come into the possession of the Macgilliechallums in the early part of the 16th century. They had pre-viously been in possession of the neighbouring lands of

Gairloch, on the mainland. The first of the family of
Raasay is said to have been Malcolm or Callum Garve
Macleod, second son of Malcolm Macleod, 8th Baron
of the Lewis. Malcolm or Gilliecallum Garve Macallaster, grandson of Callum Garve, was the first to
obtain a Crown right to the islands, having on 10th
July 1556 obtained a charter under the Government
seal. The Macleods of Raasay and the Mackenzies
were frequently at warfare. Hector Roy, the progenitor of the principal familes of the Mackenzies of
Gairloch, about the year 1511, after a bloody feud
acquired from the Siol Mhic Gilliechallum, a small
portion of their lands of Gairloch, which his successors
used, so as to become, in course of time, the proprietors
of the whole district. A massacre of the Macleods of
Raasay, in the Island of Isay, Waternish, during the
time of their chief, John Macgilliechallum, called *Ian na
Tuaidh*, the predecessor in the chieftainship of Gilliecallum Garve, served to widen the breach between the
Siol Mhic Gilliechallum, and their friends and clansmen
the Siol Torquil of Lewis on the one hand, and the
Mackenzies on the other. John Macgilliechallum of
Raasay eloped with the wife of Roderick Macleod of
Lewis, who was a daughter of John Mackenzie of Kintail, upon which Roderick divorced her, and she was
married by John, who had issue by her—several sons,
and a daughter afterwards married to Allaster Roy, a
grandson of Hector Roy Mackenzie, formerly mentioned,
which marriage gave much offence to Raasay's clan, as
they were at feud with the Mackenzies. On the death
of his first wife John of Raasay married a relation of
his own, sister of Ruari Macallan Macleod, head of the
branch of the Siol Mhic Gilliechallum, who lived in Gairloch. By this marriage John had likewise issue.
Spurred by ambition, and taking advantage of the dis-
content among the clan, Ruari Macallan plotted the
death of John of Raasay, and of his sons by the first
marriage, so that the lands of Raasay might come to
John's eldest son by the second marriage, his own

nephew.   Having brought John of Raasay, his sons by
the first marriage, and several of his nearest relations,
on invitation to the Island of Isay, as if to consult on
some important matter, Ruari procedeed to put his
sanguinary stratagem into execution.   After a sumptuous feast, which concluded the business of the day,
Ruari retired into another apartment, and causing John
and his sons to be sent for singly, he had each of them
assassinated on coming to his presence.   Ruari's plans,
however, were frustrated, for although his nephew was
nearest heir, the estates, by the assistance of the Mackenzies, became the property of Malcolm, or Gilliecallum Garve Macallaster Macleod, who obtained a crown
grant of the same, as formerly stated.   During his
minority Malcolm was put under the protection of
Campbell of Calder.   Meantime the Mackenzies sought
to punish Ruari Macallan and his assistants in revenge
for his bloody deed.   In a charter dated 1572, granted
by King James VI., failing male issue of Ruari Macleod of Lewis, remainder is granted to " Gilliecallum
Garve M'Cloyd," of Raasay, and his heir male.   In the
month of February 1588, Gilliecallum and his men,
along with the chiefs of the Mackintoshes, Mackays,
Munroes, and Macleods of Assynt, with their forces,
accompanied into Caithness the Earl of Sutherland, who
had received a commission against the Earl of Caithness,
for killing George Gordon of Marl, who had maliciously
cut the tails of the Earl of Caithness's horses.   The
people of Caithness, much alarmed at the strength of
the Earl of Sutherland's forces, fled in all directions
before him.   Several were killed and " a great prey of
cattell and goods" were taken away ; in consequence of
which the invasion was called *La na Creach mhor*, the
time of the great slaughter or spoil.   Sir Robert Gordon
writes that the invaders " brunt and wasted the toun of
Wick, but they saiffed the church, where the last Earle
of Catteynes his heart wes found in a case of lead ; the
ashes of which heart wes throwne with the wind by John
Mack Gilchalm Rasey."   A quarrel arose between the

F

said John Macgilliechalum (who was brother of Gilliecallum Garve, laird of Raasay), and Alexander Bane,
the brother of Duncan Bane of Tulloch, in Ross-shire,
in 1597, which threatened to put the shire " and all the
nighbouring cuntrie in a combustion." The Munroes
assisted the Banes, and the Mackenzies took part with
John Macgilliechallum. A skirmish between the two
forces took place at Laggiewreid, in which John Mac-
Gilliechallum and several gentlemen on both sides were
slain. The Mackenzies of Gairloch, and the Siol Mhic
Gilliechallum of Raasay, continued at variance until the
death of Gilliecallum Garve, in 1611, when the Mackenzies obtained peaceable possession of the whole lands
of Gairloch, which they still hold. Shortly after
Hector Roy had got possession of a portion of the
lands of Gairloch, as before mentioned, he or his heir
" purchased a pretended right to the whole, by some
pretence of law, which the lawfull inheritor did neglect;"
yet the Mackenzies did not venture to enforce this pretended title until the death of Torquil Dubh Macleod of
Lewis, whom the Siol Mhic Gilliechallum followed as
their superior. On the death of Torquil the Mackenzies
entered into possession of the whole of Gairloch, pursued the Siol Mhic Gilliechallum with fire and sword,
and expelled them out of Gairloch. The Siol Mhic
Gilliechallum retaliated, and invaded Gairloch " with
spoills and slaughters." Mackenzie of Gairloch apprehended John Macallan Macruari, and chased John
Holmoch Macruari, two principal men of the Macgilliechallums, at which skirmish there was slaughter on both
sides, in 1610. In the month of August of the following
year Mackenzie sent his son Murdoch, accompanied by
Alexander Bane, younger, of Tulloch, and some others,
to search for and pursue John Holmoch Macruari, and
hired a ship to convey them to Skye, where John
Holmoch was supposed to be. Either by design or
accident, the ship cast anchor in one of the harbours in
the Isle of Raasay : Gilliecallum went on board with
twelve of his guard to buy wine. When Murdoch saw

him coming, he and his followers hid themselves in the cabins of the ship, leaving the mariners only on deck. Gilliecallum transacted with the mariners and bought some wine from them, and went ashore for more boats to convey the wine to land. On his return to the ship Murdoch Mackenzie resolved to conceal himself no longer. Gilliecallum, on consulting with his men, resolved to take him prisoner in pledge of his cousin, John Macallan Macruari, detained by the laird of Gairloch. Murdoch Macgilliechallum, the laird's brother, had followed him to the ship with two galleys. A fight ensued on board the ship between the two parties, in which Murdoch Mackenzie, Alexander Bane, and all their company, with the exception of three, were slain. These three fought so manfully, that they killed the laird of Raasay with his twelve men, and wounded several of those who accompanied Murdoch Macgilliechallum in the galleys, hotly pursuing them. At last, finding themselves severely wounded, they sailed away with a fair wind, and died shortly thereafter. This event ended the strife between the two families. Gilliecallum Garve was succeeded by his son, Gilliecallum Og Macleod, or Macgilliechallum of Raasay. He was succeeded by Alexander; succeeded by John Garve, who served heir on 22d September 1648, and was married to Janet, daughter of Sir Roderick Macleod of Dunvegan. This John Garve was distinguished for his personal strength, and the gallantry of his exploits, and was accounted the strongest and best built man of his time. He met an untimely fate, having, at the early age of twenty-one, while returning from Stornoway (where he was on a visit to his uncle, Mackenzie, the Lord of Kintail), been drowned near the north coast of Skye; the vessel in which he sailed having foundered in a storm, and all on board perished. John Garve was much esteemed; and several songs were composed on the occasion of his death. His sister composed one, of which two verses may be given as a specimen :—

Iain Ghairbh Mhic Ghillechalluim
B'e mo bharantas laidir,
'N uair a rachadh tu air t-uillin,
Cha b'e uspag a gharlaoich.

'S tu fear mor do Shiol Torcuil,
'Se do chorp a bha laidir
'Nuair sheasadh iad uile
Bu leat urram nan Gaidheal.

Another lament was composed by that excellent poetess Mary Macleod, *Mari nighean Alastair Ruaidh,* which has more merit, and of which one verse may be quoted—

'Se dh' fhag 'silteach mo shuil,
Faiciun t-fhearainn gun surd,
'S do bhaile gun smuid,
Dheadh Mhic Challum nan tùr a Rarsa.

Para Mor MacCrimmon, Macleod of Macleod's piper, composed on the same occasion, that feeling *Piobaireachd,* " John Garbh Macleod of Raasay's Lament."

CHAPTER VIII.

In the time of Donald Gormeson of Sleat a fierce feud existed between the Macdonalds of Skye and the Mackenzies of Kintail. A variety of causes contributed to aggravate this feud, such as the opposition of the Mackenzies to the pretensions of the chiefs of the Macdonalds to the forfeited titles and estates of the Earldom of Ross, and Lordship of the Isles ; the death of Donald Gorme of Sleat at the siege of Elandonnan Castle ; and the two clans having taken opposite sides in the bloody disputes between Roderick Macleod, Baron of Lewis, and his reputed son Torquil Connaldagh of Cogeach, whose mother was daughter of John Mackenzie of Kintail, and the first wife of Roderick Macleod, but whom he divorced on her eloping with John Macgilliechallum of Raasay, as before stated. It then transpired that the *Breitheamh,* or Judge of the Lewis, was suspected to be the father of Torquil Connaldagh, and Roderick

consequently disowned and disinherited him.   The Mackenzies took up the cause of Torquil, their kinswoman's
son, who had married a daughter of Macdonald of
Glengarry and become a powerful warrior.   Donald
Gormeson Macdonald of Sleat (whose mother was
daughter and heiress of John Mactorquil Macleod, the
cousin and predecessor of Roderick Macleod, as Baron
of the Lewis) gave his assistance to Roderick.   Several
conflicts ensued between Roderick and Torquil, and
their dissensions were carried on for a series of years.
In the meantime (1541) Roderick Macleod married
Barbara Stewart, daughter of Andrew Lord Avandale,
by whom he had a son also named Torquil, but surnamed *Oighre*, or the Heir, to distinguish him from
Torquil Connaldagh, or Connanach, as he was sometimes styled.   Torquil Oighre grew up to be a brave
warrior, but at the early age of twenty-four, his warlike career was suddenly terminated, he having, about
the year 1566, with two hundred of his followers,
perished at sea, " by ane extraordinarie great storme
and tempest," while on their way from the Lewis to
Troternish in Skye.   Upon this event Donald Gormeson Macdonald of Sleat took steps to have himself
recognised as the next heir of the Lewis, after Roderick
Macleod, on the ground of an alleged confession of
Hugh or Uisdean, the *Breitheamh* of the Lewis, that
he was the father of Torquil Connanach.   This appears
from a protest taken by Donald Macdonald Gorme,
preserved in the charter chest of Dunvegan, dated 22d
August 1566.   Roderick Macleod of Lewis, however,
afterwards married a sister of Lachlan Maclean of
Duart, by whom he had two sons, Torquil *Dubh* and
Tormod, who afterwards contended with Torquil Connaldagh for possession of the Lewis.   Torquil Dubh
married a daughter of Tormod Macleod of Dunvegan.
In August 1569 Donald Gormeson Macdonald of Sleat
and Colin Mackenzie of Kintail were obliged in presence of the Regent and Privy Council at Perth, to
settle the quarrels in which they and their clans had

been engaged. The families thereafter continued on friendly terms, the son and heir of Donald Gormeson (Donald Gorme Mor), having married a daughter of Colin Mackenzie of Kintail. The following incident relative to the friendly terms existing between the Macdonald family and Christopher Macrae, a dependent of the Mackenzies of Kintail, and son of Macrae who shot Donald Gorme at Elandonnan, is related in a MS. history of the Macraes, written in the seventeenth century :—" Christopher was a great favourite of Macdonald, and did him a piece of service which he could not forget, which was thus—Donald Gorme Mor who was married to Mackenzie's daughter, having gone with his lady south, and staying longer than he expected, was necessitated to borrow money which he promised to pay on a certain day, and being obliged to go home in order to get the money, left his lady at Perth till his return. Meantime Christopher (who was a drover), having sold his drove and hearing that his master's daughter, Lady Macdonald, was in Perth, he went to visit her, and being informed of the cause of her stay and that of Macdonald's going home, told her he had money to answer all her demands, and men sufficient to convey her home, and advised her to clear all and set out immediately ; not doubting but she might overtake Macdonald at home, and prevent his having the trouble and risque of getting south. And so it happened, for she gladly accepted the compliment. They early next day went homewards, and having arrived the second day after Macdonald, he was greatly surprised, till the lady informed him what Christopher had done. Macdonald and his lady insisted on his staying some days, and entertained him very kindly, and on the day they were to part, Christopher being still warm with drink, called for a large cupful of strong waters, proposing, as a compliment, to drink it all to Sir Donald's good health. Macdonald, thinking himself bound to return the compliment by drinking so much to Christopher, said :—' I trust you don't mean to kill me by taking such a quantity of the liquor;' to which Christopher answered, ' Sir, and is it not natural, since it was my father that killed your father,' [should be grandfather.] While Macdonald only smiled, and said it was true, some of the bystanders, his attendants, drew their dirks, threatening to be at Christopher, and would have undoubtedly killed him, had not Sir Donald interfered, and convoyed him safe to his boat. Christopher was afterwards ashamed of what he said, but Macdonald and he continued fast friends."

In 1553 the Siol Tormod, or Macleods of Dunvegan, were placed in a position of some difficulty by the death of William Macleod, their chief, who, as formerly mentioned, left an only daughter Mary, to whom his extensive estates legally descended; but, as it was contrary to the prevailing customs and ideas to have a female in possession of the family estates, which, on her marriage, might possibly pass into the possession of a person of a rival family; the clan appears to have assisted Donald Macleod, a brother of their late chief, in seizing possession of the estates, and assuming the chieftainship. In the same year Queen Mary granted to her chancellor, George, Earl of Huntly, the nonentry and other dues of the lands of " Dunnevagane, Durynes, Brakadell, and Megynes," and of all other lands which belonged to the deceased William M'Cloid of Dunnevagane. In 1559 the Earl of Huntly resigned the grant to the Queen Regent, Mary of Guise, who then sold to James Macdonald of Dunnyveg, Islay, the nonentry and other dues of the lands of Mary M'Cloide, the heiress of William M'Cloide. Donald Macleod did not retain his illegal possession of these lands; having, in 1557, been assassinated at Kingsburgh by a relation of his own, John Oig Macleod, who, failing Tormod, Donald's only brother, would have become the male representative of the family. He unsuccessfully plotted against the life of Tormod, who was at the time attending the University of Glasgow. He contrived to retain possession of the estates until his death in 1559, when Tormod assumed the chieftainship, and possession of the estates, though having no legal title to do so. In 1562 the person of Mary Macleod was in the custody of Kenneth Mackenzie of Kintail, who, having refused to give her up to James Macdonald of Dunnyveg (who was appointed by the Regent as her guardian), was at length compelled to deliver her to Queen Mary, with whom she remained for some years as a maid of honour, and is supposed to have been one of the Queen's celebrated *Maries.* Archibald, Earl of Argyle, acquired the ward of Mary Macleod from James Macdonald, and gave her in marriage to his kinsman Duncan Campbell, younger, of Auchinbreck. In 1567 he bound himself by a contract with Tormod Macleod, to procure his infeftment in the lands of Mary Macleod, and her surrender of the same, on condition of Tormod paying £1000 towards the dowery of his niece. He also became bound to obtain for Donald Macdonald Gorme of Sleat, heritable infeftment in the lands of Troternish, and others, to be held of Queen Mary, on condition that Donald should pay one thousand marks, Scots, to the Earl, and five hundred towards the dowery of Mary Macleod, and should give his bond of manrait, or service, for himself and his clan to the Earl. In 1572 King James VI., at the request of the Earl of Argyle, and on the narrative that some of the charters of the lands, which formerly belonged to Alexander Macleod of Dunvegan, had been destroyed in the local wars, granted these lands in heritage to Mary Macleod, which, with consent of her husband, she resigned in 1580, and the same were granted by King James to Tormod Macleod, who was then infeft therein. Tormod Macleod was married to Giles, daughter of Hector Maclean of Duart, by his wife Lady Janet Campbell, daughter of Archibald, Earl of Argyle, and by her had three sons—William his heir, Roderick (afterwards Sir Roderick), and Alexander of Minginish—and a daughter, Margaret, who married Donald Macdonald of Sleat. In 1572 the lands of " Wattirness," in Skye, were resigned by " Roderick

Makcloyd of Lewis," and were granted by King James
VI. to his son, and apparent heir "Torquil Makcloyd,
and his male heirs, with remainder to Gillecallum
Garwe M'Cloyd of Raisay, and his male heirs, and to
Torquil's male heirs whomsoever bearing the M'Cloid
surname and arms, reserving the liferent to Roderick,
and on condition that he and Torquil should commit no
crime against the King." A yearly pension of 1000
marks, Scots, out of the fruits of the Bishoprick of
Aberdeen, then vacant, was conferred by the King in
the same year on Donald Gormeson of Sleat, for his
good and faithful service. About the year 1578 John,
son and heir of James Macdonald Gruamach of Castle
Camus, in Sleat, who was kept prisoner in the castle of
Inchconnell, Lochawe, made complaint against the
Earl of Argyle for oppressive and illegal conduct in de-
taining him prisoner. This John became the father of
a well-known warrior of the Macdonalds—Donald Mac-
Ian Mhic Sheumais—and his imprisonment by Argyle
is referred to in a song composed to Donald—

A mhic an Eoin eucaich bha geimhlibh Mhic Chalein.

In 1581 King James VI. " granted to John, bishop of
the Isles, the escheat of all the goods belonging to the
deceased Donald M'Gillespie Clereische, bailie of
Trouterness, Huchoun M'Gillaspie, his brother, Malan-
eill Maknicoll, 'officiar' of Trouternes, Nicoll, his
brother, and others who were all denounced rebels, and
at the horn for not paying the fermas and dues belonging to the bishoprick of the Isles, and the abbey of Icolmkill."

Tormod Macleod of Dunvegan died in 1584, and on
31st July of the following year his son William was
served heir. William Macleod married Janet Mackintosh, daughter of Mackintosh of Mackintosh. They
had no issue, and on his death in 1590 he was succeeded
by his brother Roderick Macleod, afterwards Sir
Roderick, and better known in tradition as *Ruari Mor.*
Donald *Gormeson* of Sleat died in 1585, and was suc-

ceeded by his son, Donald *Gorme Mor,* a powerful warrior, and no mean diplomatist. He entered into a treasonable correspondence with Queen Elizabeth of England. In a letter to her, dated March 1598, preserved in the State Paper Office, he styles himself " Lord of the Isles of Scotland, and chief of the Clandonald Irishmen ;" and offers upon certain " reasonable motives and considerations" to inform her of the movements of her enemies in Scotland, to persuade the Isles to throw off all allegiance to the Scottish Crown, and to raise an insurrection to *fasche* King James. He would also disclose Scottish practices, and how the Northern Jesuits and priests pushed forward their diabolical, pestiferous, and anti-christian courses. His services were not, however, accepted. He had scarcely assumed the chieftainship of the Clan Donald, when, through the treachery of two of his kinsmen, *Huisdean Macghilleasbuig Chlerach* and *Macdhomnull Herrach,* he was plunged into one of those bloody feuds so common at the period, and which at length became so widespread and serious as to call for the interference of Government. The circumstances which led to this feud are narrated by Sir Robert Gordon as follows :— " Donald Gorme Macdonald of Slait, trawelling from the Yle of Sky, to visit his cousin, Angus Macdonald of Kintyre (or Keantire), landed with his train in ane yland called Juray, or Duray, which pairtlie apperteyned to Angus Macdonald, and pairtlie to Sir Laughlane Macklain. And by chance he fortuned to land in that pairt of the yland which apperteyneth to Macklain, being driven in thither by contrary winds, wher they were no sooner on shoar, but Macdonald Tearragh and Houcheon Mackgillespick (two of the Clandonald who had latelie fallen out with Donald Gorme), arryved their also with a company of men, and vnderstanding that Donald Gorme wes their, they secreitlie took away, by night, a number of cattell out of that pairt of the iland which apperteaned to Macklain ; and so they retire agane to the sea, thinking thereby to stur up a tumult in the

iland against Donald Gorme, by making the Clanlain
to believe that this wes done by Donald Gorme and his
men—which fell out accordinglie. For Donald Gorme
and his company, lying at a place in the iland called
Inverchuockwrick, wer suddently invaded unawars,
under silence of the night (neither suspecting nor expecting any such interteynment), by Sir Laughlane
Macklain, and his tryb the Macklain, who had assembled
ther whole forces againes them. Macklain killed that
night about thriescore of the Clandonald. Donald
Gorme himselff escaped by going that night to sleip in
a ship that lay in the harbor. · Heiropon ther arose
great troubles betuein the Clandonald and the Clanlain,
which did not end vntill the death of this Sir Laghlane
Macklain, who wes slain afterward by Sir James
Mackonald, his owne sister's sone, and the sone of the
foresaid Angus, the yeir of God 1598.''

Donald Gorme returned at once to Skye, much
enraged at what he believed such an unprovoked
attack, and determined upon taking active measures
of vengeance against the Macleans. These feelings
rapidly spread amongst all the Macdonalds and their
allies. Violent measures of retaliation were immediately resorted to, and carried to such an extent, that on
18th September 1585, King James VI. wrote Roderick
Macleod of Dunvegan, earnestly requesting that chief
to assist Maclean of Duart against the Clandonald,
who had already done much injury to Maclean and his
followers, and threatened to do more. In the meantime Angus Macdonald of Islay, hearing of the unfortunate occurrence between his brother-in-law, Sir
Lachlan Maclean, and his cousin, Donald Gorme, went
to Skye to consult with Donald Gorme and attempt
to bring about a reconciliation with Maclean. " After
that Angus had remained a whyle in the Skye with his
cousen, he taketh journey homeward into Kintyre, and
in his return, he landed in the Yle of Mule, and went to
the castle of Duart; Macklain, his principall duelling
in Mulle, against the advyse and opinion of his tuo

brethern, Coll Mack James and Reynald Mack James, and of his cowsen Reynald MackColl, who did earnestly persuad him to the contrarie, desireing him to send some gentleman of his train vnto Macklain, to declare vnto him how he had sped with his cousen, Donald Gorme, and how far he wes inclyned to a reconciliation vpon a reasonable satisfaction. But Angus trusted so much to his brother-in-law, Sir Laghlan Macklain, that he wold not hearken vnto their councell, wherevpon his tuo brethren left him; bot his cousen, Renald Mack-Coll, accompanied him to Duart, wher Angus and all his company wer perfidiously taken prisoners by Sir Laghlan Macklain, the nixt day after ther arryval, Renald MackColl only escaping, and that verie hardlie." Angus Macdonald was detained there in captivity, until, to preserve his life, he agreed to renounce in favour of Maclean, the lands of Rinns of Islay, the possession of which was long disputed between the two clans, and had to leave his eldest son, James Macdonald, and his brother, Ranald Macjames, as pledges with Maclean until he should get the title of the Rinns; whereupon Angus Macdonald regained his liberty, but seeing how he had been wronged by Maclean, he returned to his castle meditating revenge against Maclean for his treatment of himself and of his kinsman, Donald Gorme. Thereupon followed a series of treacherous seizures and raids, accompanied by much bloodshed on both sides, in which the Clanranald, Clanian, Clanleod of Lewis, Macneills of Eiglia, Macallasters, and Macfies, joined the Macdonalds, and the Clanleod of Dunvegan and Harris, Macneills of Barra, Mackinnons, and Macquarries, joined the Macleans. Sir Lachlan Maclean also hired a hundred Spanish soldiers, who were on board the "Florida," one of the vessels of the Spanish Armada, and with them he plundered and ravaged the Isles of Rum, Canna, and Eig. This disastrous feud was only put an end to on Donald Gorme Mor Macdonald of Sleat, Angus Macdonald of Islay, and Sir Lachlan Maclean, while in Edinburgh on the invitation of the King and Council, being seized and imprisoned in the Castle, where they were detained until they paid fines imposed by the King, and procured sureties for their future peaceful conduct. This happened in the year 1591. The fine imposed on Donald Gorme Mor was £4000. John Campbell of Calder became surety for his future obedience to law and order, which included his good behaviour towards the Government of Queen Elizabeth in Ireland. Campbell of Calder was assassinated in 1592, at the instigation of two of his countrymen, Campbell of Glenurchy, and Campbell of Ardkinlass. Upon this event Donald Gorme Mor felt himself somewhat relieved from his obligations to the Government, which he failed to perform, and was preparing his galleys and collecting his men for a military adventure into Ireland. He was summoned to appear before the Privy Council, but failed to do so; and in 1593 he was summoned to appear before Parliament, on charges of treason and lese majesty. He was, however, not the least put about by these legal forms, but in company with his neigh-bour, *Ruari Mor* Macleod of Dunvegan, set out in their galleys for Ireland, each having five hundred warriors of his clan under his command. They went to the assistance of Red Hugh, the chief of the ancient race of O'Donnells, in his rebellion against Queen Elizabeth. They landed at Lough Foyle, where they were entertained by O'Donnell for three days and three nights, after which Donald Gorme Mor returned to Skye, leaving his brother in command of his men. Ruari Mor remained in person with his followers.

CHAPTER IX.

THERE are many tales related of the exploits of Donald Gorme's treacherous kinsman Hugh or Huisdean Macgilleasbuig Chlerach, besides the unfortunate affair at

Jura.   He was a man of great personal strength
(" B'eutrom a cheum, Bu trom a bhuille,") to which he
added cruelty and deceit.   He at first possessed the
confidence of his kinsman Donald Gorme, who sent
him as factor to North Uist.   Finding on his arrival
there that a family of the name of Macvicar *(Clann a
Phiocar Mhor)*, held lands which he considered should
be in the possession of his own near relatives he put to
death four brothers of the Macvicars, each of whom
possessed a dun and farm.   Their sister composed a
lament for them, still preserved as a waulking song.
It closes with an imprecation on the cruel Hugh, which
may be translated, though imperfectly, thus :—

> O Hugh ! thou son of Archie Clerk,
> May thy strong frame grow stiff and stark,
> Thy red blood stain thy shirt of mail—
> The maids of Sleat hear thy death-tale.
>
> Ill luck betide thy foster nurse,
> That did not in her arms thee crush
> While yet a suckling, weak and small,
> Ere thou didst slay my brethren all.

Donald Gorme permitted Hugh to build a residence for
himself at Cuidrach, Skye.   Hugh erected a strong fort
there at the seaside, the ruins of which still receive the
name of *Caisteal Huisdean,* Hugh's castle.   When this
stronghold was about finished, Donald Gorme dis-
covered that Hugh plotted the destruction of his chief
and the leading men of· the clan at the house-warming
he intended to give, in order that he himself might
assume the chieftainship.   On finding that his plot
had been found out, Hugh at once set off in his galley
to North Uist, to escape the vengeance of his chief.
It is said that while there he wrote a letter to Donald
Gorme, in which he made professions of his fidelity
and affection for him, and another letter to William
Martin, residing at the Eastside of Troternish, a tenant
of Donald Gorme's, and a man of some power and
influence, in which he disclosed a plot against his chief
and asking Martin's assistance.   By some mishap
Martin's letter was addressed to Donald Gorme, and

Donald Gorme's to Martin.   On receiving this fresh instance of the treachery of Hugh, Donald Gorme sent a strong party to seize him.   After having evaded his pursuers for a long time, they at last succeeded in apprehending him in *Dun a Sticir,* and carried him prisoner to Skye.   He occupied Dun-a-Sticir alone, and was maintained there by the kindness of a lady, who went once a day to the Dun with food.   The Dun is in the middle of a lake and is reached by stepping stones. Hugh was polite enough to see the lady safely over the stepping stones when she visited him, and it was while in this act that his pursuers succeeded in securing him. He was imprisoned by Donald Gorme in a vaulted dungeon in his castle of Duntulm, where he was allowed to die of thirst, in the horrid agonies of which he crunched an empty pewter jug, left in his cell, to powder.

In the Parliament of 1593, the Lord Advocate produced the third summons of treason against Donald Gorme Mor, (who is styled " Donald M'Coneil Gorme of Sleatt,") and other Hebridean chieftains for the crimes of treason and lese majesty.   In June 1596 Donald Gorme Mor made his submission to King James VI.   He was restored into favour and recognised as the heir of Hugh of Sleat.   On this occasion he procured a lease from the Crown of the district of Troternish. Angus Macdonald of Islay, in making his submission to the King shortly thereafter, craves his Majesty that he (Angus) " be reasonablie and friendlie handlit, as hes bein done to Donald Gorum."   Rory Mor of Dunvegan also made his submission to the King about this time.   He was infeft as heir to his brother William in the family estates, upon a precept from Chancery in September of that year,   A letter from him in which he styles himself *Rodericus MacCloid of the Herrie,* addressed " To his Hynes Maiestie Soverane Lord, King and Maister" James, the *sapient and sext,* and dated from Marvak, Harris, the 22d September 1596, is very characteristic.   The letter acknowledges delivery of a charge from the King on the 18th September, commanding him to be at Islay, with his force, on the 20th day of the said month, under the pains of treason, " quhilk charge (he writes) I taik God and your Grace to wutness giff it wes possible to me to haive done the samen ; althocht my force haid beine togidder, and wund and weddir haid serued me at eiverie airt of the broken seis in the cuntreis, and my men lye far sindrie ; and althocht the chairge haid beine giffin to me the first of August, it haid beine lytle aneuche to haive beine at the day apoyntit with my force. Sir, I beseik your Grace think nocht this to be ane excuiss. I will ly all this asyd, and althocht I sould be borne in ane horse litter, I sall do my exact diligence to be at my Lord Crowner quhair your Grace has commandit me in all possible haist, as I sall answer to God and your Grace baith, and quhome your Grace or my Lord Crowner will command me in your Hienes' name to pass on, ather be sword or fyre, I sall do the same, or ony your Grace will command me to feacht hand in hand in your Grace sight, I sall prove my pithe on him. Beseikand your Grace faivorably to lat not vse me withe letters of tressoun nor treatorie, I beine in mynd to serwe your Grace vnder God as my native king and maister to the utermaist of my lyfe. This wayadge beine endit, I will rejoce to be at your Grace and to haive your Grace presens, and to serwe and knaw your Grace as my only soverane, king, lord, and maister : luiking for your Grace's answere giff neid beis againe with this berar, to haive your Gracis presens, and God bliss your Grace."

In 1597 an Act of Parliament was passed, making it imperative on all landlords and chieftains in the Highlands and Isles to exhibit their title deeds before the Lords of Exchequer, upon the 15th May 1598, and to find security for the payment of the Crown rents, and their future peaceable behaviour, under the pain of forfeiture of their titles. It appears the Skye chiefs considered themselves justified in resisting this arbitary enactment, the consequence of which was that the islands of Lewis and Harris, the lands of Dunvegan in Skye, and Glenelg on the mainland, were declared to be at the disposal of the Government. The Island of Lewis and the district of Troternish were granted to a company of adventurers,—chiefly gentlemen of Fife-shire. They were to be free from the payment of rent for seven years, after which they were annually to pay 140 chalders of bere for the Lewis, and 400 merks for Troternish. The adventurers assembled in Fife in October 1599, where they collected a company of soldiers and artificers of all sorts, with everything which they thought necessary for a plantation. They proceeded to the Lewis and built the town of Stornoway. They, however, met with so much opposition from the Macleods of Lewis, who were secretly assisted by Donald Gorme Mòr, Rory Mòr, and Mackenzie of Kintail, that they were ultimately forced to abandon their undertaking in the Lewis, and the colonization of Troternish and of Harris, Dunvegan, and Glenelg, which were also granted to them, they did not attempt.

CHAPTER X.

A SUDDEN quarrel at this time unfortunately took place between Donald Gorme Mòr and Rory Mòr, which plunged their clans into a fierce feud against each other, which feud was accompanied by much bloodshed and pillaging, calling at length, in 1601, for the special attention of the Government. Donald Gorme Mòr had married Margaret Macleod, sister of Rory Mòr, but " for some displeasure or jealousy conceived against her, he did repudiate her." It is related that the sight of one of the lady's eyes was affected, and that Donald Gorme, to shew her all the indignity that he could, sent her back to Dunvegan, mounted on a one-eyed grey horse, led by a one-eyed lad, and followed by a terrier, also blind of an eye. Rory Mòr at first sent

Donald Gorme a civil message to take his wife back; but Donald not only refused to do so, but applied for a divorce against her, on procuring which he married the sister of Kenneth Mackenzie, Lord of Kintail. Rory Mòr was so offended at this insult, that he assembled his clan and invaded the district of Troternish with fire and sword. Donald Gorme, in revenge, collected his forces and invaded Macleod's lands of Harris, killing some of the inhabitants, and carrying away a great booty of cattle. This so roused Rory Mòr, that with the warriors of his clan he sailed for the Island of North Uist, belonging to Donald Gorme, and landing in the north part of the Island, he sent his cousin, Donald *Glas* Macleod, with forty men to spoil the Island, and (according to Sir Robert Gordon) "to tak a prey of goods out of the precinct of the church of Killtrynad, wher the people had put all ther goods and cattle as in a sanctuarie," that here they were encountered by a kinsman of Donald Gorme's (Donald *MacIain Mhic Sheumais*), with twelve men, who fought so valiantly, that they not only rescued the cattle and goods, but killed Donald *Glas*, with the most of his party. The local tradition of the battle narrates that it was the Macleods, after having succeeded in raising the *creach* of the Island, that had gathered their booty into the church, or monastery of the Trinity at Carinish, and that they were feasting there on some of their plunder, when Donald MacIain Mhic Sheumais arrived with his twelve warriors, who fought with their bows and arrows and swords with such effect, that only two of the Macleods escaped to convey the news of their discomfiture to their chief, who was with his galleys at Portnalong. Donald MacIain Mhic Sheumais received a severe arrow wound in the action, from which he, however, soon recovered, and continued to distinguish himself as a warrior. The leader of the Macleods was slain by a Macdougall named Donald *Mor MacNeil MhicIain*, at the sands named from that circumstance, *Ottir Mhic-Dhomhnuil Ghlais*. The slain of the party were buried at the scene of the action, known as *Feitheadh-na-fola,* or the morass of blood, and their sculls were placed in the windows of the church of the Trinity, where they were to be seen up to a recent date. Rory Mòr, seeing the bad success of his clansmen, and suspecting that there were greater forces in the Island, retired home, intending to return shortly with greater forces to avenge his loss.

In about three weeks Donald MacIain Mhic Sheumais was sufficiently recovered to proceed to Skye to report the affair at Carinish personally to his chief, Donald Gorme Mòr. He accordingly set sail in his galley with a befitting retinue, but when about half way across the Minch, which separates North Uist and the other islands of the outer Hebrides from Skye, a violent snow storm with contrary wind arose, so that Donald was driven back, and had no recourse but to make for Rodil, in Harris, one of the seats of his enemy Rory Mòr. It was dark when Donald and his company landed, and their arrival was known to no one at Rodil with the exception of Macleod's page, Maccrimmon, a native of Skye, to whom Donald stood in the relation of *goistidh,* or godfather. Rory Mòr, as usual, had a number of the gentlemen of his clan waiting on and feasting with him at Rodil House. The severity of the storm made the chief uneasy. He paced to and fro in his dining-hall, and removing the panel from one of the apertures that served as windows, he peered into the darkness without, and shuddered as the blast blew in through the window a shower of snow. Hastily closing the aperture he exclaimed, " I would not refuse shelter to my greatest enemy, even Donald MacIain Mhic Sheumais, on such a night." Maccrimmon immediately answers " I take you at your word, Donald MacIain Mhic Sheumais is here." Rory Mòr was rather taken aback by the unexpected announcement, but yielding to no man in hospitality, he at once requested that Donald and his company be shown in. The Macdonalds entered, and after a formal salutation,

were requested to sit down to dinner with their host
and his kinsmen.   The long table groaned under its
burden of beef, venison, and salmon.   The Macleods were
seated on one side, and the Macdonalds ranged themselves on the other side of the table, the dunevassals
of either clan being seated above, and the vassals below
the salt.   Abundance of good old wine was quaffed,
and as it took effect, the Macleods, who did not appear
to relish the presence of the strangers, cast furtive
glances across the table.   At length the murmured
and listless conversation was interrupted by the words
" Remember ! This day three weeks was fought the
battle of Carinish," spoken by one of the Macleods, in
a loud and emphatic tone.   The chief gave a frowning
look to the speaker, but that did not deter him from
repeating the unfortunate words, which acted as a live
spark on the combustible nature of the Macleods, and
in an instant they displayed a score of daggers.   A
bloody scene would have inevitably followed had not
the chief at once interfered, and with a voice of authority commanded his hasty clansmen to sheath their
weapons, and not disgrace his hospitality and their own
gallantry by such an ill-timed act.   They at once
obeyed, and he apologised to Donald for his clansmen's
rashness, and good humouredly enquired of him why
he had unsheathed his sword.   Donald replied that he
did not mean to act on the offensive, but that if any of
his men had been struck he intended to have secured first
the highest bird in the air, " *an t-eun as airde tha 'san
ealtuin.*"   When the hour for retiring came, the Macdonalds were shown to an outer house to sleep, but
Donald, as being of higher rank, was about being
shown to a bed-room in the house, when he declined to
go, preferring to accompany his men, which he did.
They retired to rest, but had scarcely slept, when Maccrimmon came to the door and called to Donald Mac
Iain Mhic Sheumais that there was now fair wind for
Skye.   The Macdonalds at once got up, and finding
that the gale had subsided and the wind was favour-

able, they embarked in their galley for Skye. They had scarcely reached the entrance of the bay of Rodil when on looking back they observed the dormitory they had left in flames, some of the Macleods having treacherously set it on fire, suspecting that the Macdonalds were within. The piper of the Macdonalds struck up the piobaireachd " *Tha an dubhthuil air Macleod*," *i.e.*, the Macleods are disgraced, which galled the Macleods on perceiving that they were outwitted. The Macdonalds were soon borne by the breeze to their destination, Duntulm, in Troternish.

In the absence of Rory Mòr in Argyle, seeking the aid and advice of the Earl of Argyle against the Macdonalds, in 1601, Donald Gorme Mòr assembled his men and made an invasion into Macleod's lands, desiring to force on a battle. Alexander Macleod of Mingnish, the brother of Rory Mòr, collected all the fighting men of the Siol Tormad, and some of the Siol Torquil, and encamped by Ben Chullin. Next day they and the Macdonalds joined battle, " which continued all the day long, both contending for the victory with incredible obstinacy." The leader of the Macleods (who was cased in armour) together with Niel MacAlister Roy, and thirty of the leading men of the Macleods were wounded and taken prisoners, and the Macdonalds succeeded in gaining the battle. John Mactormod, and Tormod Mactormod, two near kinsmen of Rory Mòr, and several others of the Macleods, were slain. Donald MacIain Mhic Sheumais fought with great bravery in the action under Donald Gorme Mòr. The ravine where the battle was fought is hence named *Coire na creach*, or the ravine of the spoil. The Privy Council now interfered, and requested the chiefs to disband and quit Skye. Donald Gorme Mòr was ordered to surrender himself to the Earl of Huntly, and Rory Mòr to the Earl of Argyle, and were charged to remain with these noblemen under the pain of treason, until the quarrel between them should be settled by the King and Council. Through the media-

tion of Angus Macdonald of Cantyre, the Laird of
Coll, and other friends, a reconciliation was effected
between them, upon which Donald Gorme Mòr delivered
up to Rory Mòr the prisoners taken at Ben Chullin,
after which they refrained from open hostility, though
they did have actions of law against each other.   On
the reconciliation being effected, Donald Gorme Mòr
was invited by Rory Mòr to a banquet in Dunvegan
Castle.   When Donald Gorme Mòr appeared in sight
of the castle he was met by Macleod's splendid piper,
Donald Mòr Maccrimmon, who welcomed the chief of
the Macdonalds by playing "The Macdonald's Salute,"
which *piobaireachd* he composed for the occasion.   It
was at the same banquet that he composed " *Failte nan
Leodach.*"   This Donald Mòr Maccrimmon had a brother
named *Padruie Caog,* who was piper on Macleod's lands
of Glenelg.   He was assassinated by a Kintail man, in
revenge for which Donald Mòr went to Kintail to
avenge his death.   The inhabitants of the village in
which the offender resided refused to deliver him up,
upon which Donald Mòr set fire to several of their
houses, causing the loss of some lives.   He escaped to
Lord Rea's country, and lived for some time under the
protection of Donald Duaghal Mackay, afterwards Lord
Rea.   Mackenzie 'of Kintail (whose daughter was
married to Mackay), sent his son and twelve men in
search of Donald Mòr, who on hearing of their arrival
betook to the hills, occasionally visiting a shepherd's
house.   Mackenzie and his men came there on one
occasion while Donald Mòr was in bed.   It had been
raining, and the shepherd's wife took the wet plaids
of the visitors and spread them across the house on
a rope, under cover of which Donald made his escape.
During the night he returned to the house when the
inmates were asleep, and he took Mackenzie's arms
and part of those of his men, and piled them up close
to where Mackenzie lay.   He then left the house without disturbing any one.   When Mackenzie awoke in
the morning and found his arms so placed, he called to

his men to get up, saying, " I might have been a dead man for aught you could have done for me. If Donald Mòr Maccrimmon is alive it was he did this, and it was as easy a matter for him to take my life as to do so." On going out they saw Donald on the other side of a river, with his great sword in his hand, and they were about fording the river with the intention of killing him, when Mackenzie threatened to shoot the first man that would touch him. He then desired Donald to come across. " No," replied he, " it is as easy for you to come to me as for me to go to you." Mackenzie pledged his word of honour that he would not be injured if he came. Donald replied " Swear all your men and I will take your own word." This was done, and Donald instead of being taken prisoner, held a friendly interview with Mackenzie, who promised to procure his pardon, which he did, and Donald returned by Kintail to Skye, where he continued in his capacity as Macleod's piper until his death, when he was succeeded by Patrick or Para Mòr Maccrimmon, who was a no less famous piper. He composed more pipe music or *piobaireachds*, than any other piper of whom there is account. Seven of his sons died in course of one year. It was on that occasion he composed the feeling and mournful *piobaireachd* " *Cumha na Cloinne*," or the Children's Lament.

After his peace with Rory Mòr, Donald Gorme Mòr went to visit John, Earl of Sutherland, to Sutherland, and there renewed the ancient league and friendship contracted between their predecessors.

CHAPTER XI.

ON 12th July 1606, Sir Lauchlan Mackinnon of Strath (who was knighted by James VI.) entered into a bond of friendship with the chief of the Macnabs, Finlay Macnab of Bowaine. Mackinnon's signature to the Bond is " Lauchland *Mise* MacFingon." The Mackin-

nons and Macnabs were branches of the Clan Alpine,
and though residing at considerable distance from each
other, they maintained friendly relations, as did also the
Macgregors, who were of the Clan Alpine.   At a later
period (1671) the chief of Mackinnon entered into a
bond with Macgregor of Macgregor, "faithfully to
serve one another in all causes, with their men and
servants, against all who live or die."

In 1608, on account of the irregularity of the chiefs,
in the.Western Isles, in paying the King's rents, and
of the frequent disturbances that took place there, King
James appointed Lord Ochiltree as Lieutenant over the
Isles, with power to him and his council, of which
Andrew Knox, Bishop of the Isles, was president, to
treat with the Islanders to demolish such castles as they
thought fit, to destroy the galleys and birlings in the
Isles, and to place garrisons in some of the castles.
Ochiltree appointed the Island chiefs to meet him at
the castle of Aros in Mull, where several of them
appeared, among whom were Donald Gorme Mòr of
Sleat, Rory Mòr of Dunvegan, and Alexander Macleod,
his brother.   As they did not quite agree to Ochiltree's
proposals, at the suggestion of the Bishop he invited the
assembled chiefs on board His Majesty's ship 'Moon,'
to hear a sermon from the Bishop, after which he prevailed on them to dine, and they had hardly finished
their feasting, when, to their astonishment and dismay,
they were informed that they were prisoners by the
King's order, and were accordingly conveyed to the
castles of Dumbarton, Blackness, and Stirling, as
prisoners.   Rory Mòr of Dunvegan alone refused to
enter the vessel, suspecting Ochiltree's motives.   Some
months thereafter Donald Gorme Mòr of Sleat was
liberated on finding security for his return to Edinburgh
by a certain day, and for his concurrence and assistance
to the Bishop, in making a survey of the Isles.   In the
summer of 1609 the Bishop made his survey, and held
a court in Iona, of the chiefs and gentlemen of the Isles,
at which the nine "Statutes of Icolmkill," for the

improvement of the Isles, were enacted. These acts provided for the increase of the clergy, the promotion of education, the establishment of inns, the suppression of drunkenness and the use of fire-arms, and the repression of bards, followers, and vagrants. The three Skye chiefs, Donald Gorme Mòr, Rory Mòr, and Mackinnon, were present at this court.

In 1613 Rory Mòr Macleod of Dunvegan, Harris, and Glenelg, was knighted by King James, and on 16th June, 1616, he received a particular license from his Majesty to go to London, to the Court, at any time he pleased. In July 1610 Sir Rory Mòr purchased from Kenneth Mackenzie, Lord Kintail, the lands and barony of Vaterness (Waternish), consisting of five *unciate,* which had previously belonged to the Macleods of Lewis. In a description of Skye, written about this time, mention is made of " the country cald Vatirnes perteyning to Mackloyd of Harray, being of old the possession of Macloyd of Lewis. It is thirty-two merk land, that is four daachs of land." The same writer describes Troternish as having " dyvers paroche kirks," and being " fertil of corne pasture and fishing." The Isle of Scalpay, which was at this time held by Maclean of Dirvart, is mentioned in the same account as having " a church and church toun," and being " plentifull of deir which doth much harme among the corne landis. It hath also wild sheep, which ever keep the fields contrair to the use of those countreys." Another description of Skye, written about the same period, gives the following statement as to its genial climate :—" This Isle is blest with a good and temperate air, which, though sometimes foggy, and the hills often surrounded with mist, so that they can scarce be discerned, yet the summer, by reason of the continuall and gentle winds, so abating the heat and the thickness of the air—yet frequent showers in the winter so asswageing the cold, that neither the one nor the other proves obnoxious to the inhabitants, the summer not scorching, nor the winter benumming them." The same description gives

a very favourable account of the habits and character of
the inhabitants—their hospitality to strangers, their
veneration for their chiefs and king, their activity in
field sports, and their taste for poetry, music, and tradition.   The females are described as "verie modest,
temperet in their dyet and apparell, excessively grieved
at the death of any near relation."   Protestantism must
have made considerable progress in the Island, for the
inhabitants are described as honouring " ther ministers
in a high degree, to whose care, under God, they owe
ther freedom from idolatrie, and many superstitious
customes."

By a letter dated " At Quhythall, the fifth day of
November 1611," King James granted to Andrew,
Bishop of the Isles, " all and quhatsumever soumes of
money sall be found rest and auentand to his Majestie,
by Donald Gorme of Slaitte, Rorye MacCloyd of Hereis,
Lauchlane Mackennie of Strathorrodill, Alexander Mac-
Gillichallom of Rasa," and other Highland chiefs
therein mentioned, " for yair parties of quhatsomever
taxationes, grantit to his Majestie, within his said
kingdom, at any tim preceeding the first day of July
1606."   In July 1613, Donald Gorme Mòr of Sleat, and
Sir Rory Mòr of Dunvegan, are mentioned as having
settled with the Exchequer, and as continuing in their·
obedience to the laws.

The bravery of Donald MacIain Mhic Sheumais in
fighting in behalf of his chief and kinsman Donald
Gorme Mòr of Sleat, has been already referred to.   In
the " Douglas Baronage" he is described as " a man of
extraordinary courage and great strength of body.   He
commanded the Macdonalds in three set battles against
the invaders of his country."   In acknowledgment of
these services Donald Gorme Mòr conferred on him
the lands of ℒ :drach in Troternish.   His activity in
peaceful pursuits, after the quarrel between the Skye
chiefs was settled, was no less marked, for he was the
first man who ventured to take a drove of cows from
Skye to the south country, and he continued until of

advanced age to be an extensive cattle-dealer. He became the ancestor of the Macdonalds of Kingsburgh, having married a daughter of Macdonald of Keppoch, by whom he had a numerous family. His eldest son was Alexander Macdonald of Kingsburgh, who married Margaret, a niece of Sir Donald Macdonald ot Sleat. Donald MacIain Mhic Sheumais's daughter Mary was married to Mac Mhic Thormaid or Macleod of Gesto ; a proud and high-tempered gentleman, but kind withal. Macleod on occasions twitted his wife on the homely pursuit her father had taken to, whom he named *Aireach liath nam bo,* or the grey cowfeeder. Macleod's sister was married to Maccaskill of Ebost, and on the occasion of the birth of a son to Maccaskill, Macleod went to congratulate him. Over their punch at night the brothers-in-law disputed. From high words they came to use their weapons, Maccaskill raised his sword to cleave Macleod's skull, but the point of the sword stuck in the rafter or wooden beam above him, and Macleod seeing the sword raised above his head plunged his dagger into Maccaskill's breast, making a mortal wound. Macleod at once returned home, told his wife what had occurred, and asked her advice what he should do, as he was sure the Maccaskills of Rhundunan would be on his track to take vengeance for Ebost's death. She advised him to go to *Airiach liath nam bo* for protection. Though this step was somewhat humiliating, he at once set out for Cuidrach, and was received by his father-in-law. On the morrow a party of Maccaskills were descried on a height above Cuidrach House ; Macleod remained in the house, and Donald MacIain Mhic Sheumais, having his large broadsword, walked to and fro in front of the house as guard. The Maccaskills sent a boy whom they had taken as guide. to the house, to ask that the murderer should be put out. He was terrified at Donald MacIain Mhic Sheumais's wild appearance, who asked him his message and what was his name. The boy, who was a Macdonald, answered. Mhic Sheumais told him it was a good thing for him he was a Macdonald, otherwise he had forfeited his life, that Macleod would not be delivered up, and that if the Maccaskills had any value for their lives they better not attempt to secure him. The boy returned with this message, and informed the Maccaskills how frightened he was at the grey-haired giant-looking man who met him, and who used his large sword as a walking-stick. Upon this the Maccaskills prudently determined that as their deceased kinsman and Macleod were related, there was no call on them to risk their lives to revenge his death, and they consequently returned to their homes.

CHAPTER XII.

In 1616, Sir Rory Mòr Macleod of Dunvegan, and Sir Lauchlan Mackinnon of Strath, appeared before the Privy Council. Macleod was taken bound to appear annually before the Council on the 10th July, and exhibit three of his principal kinsmen.   He was allowed to keep only six gentlemen in his household, and have Dunvegan Castle as his fixed residence, where his consumption of wine for the use of the household was limited to four tuns a year.   Mackinnon was taken bound to exhibit one of his kinsmen annually before the Council, but he gave up the names of five disobedient clansmen, for whose conduct he would not be responsible. His residence was fixed at Kilmorie in Strath, and he was allowed to have three household gentlemen, and consume one tun of wine.   Donald Gorme Mòr of Sleat was prevented by illness from attending the Council, but he named Duntulm Castle as his principal residence, and was allowed six gentlemen for his retinue, and a consumption of four tuns of wine a year. The chiefs were further taken bound to free their estates of sturdy beggars and idlers, and to let what lands they did not themselves cultivate to tenants at fixed rents, instead of service and other exactions, to make " policie and planting" about their houses, and to cultivate home farms. They were limited to the use of "one birling, or galley, of sixteen or eighteen oars" each, and none but the chiefs and their household gentlemen were permitted to wear swords, or carry arms, except when engaged in the King's service. In the same year Donald Gorme Mòr Macdonald of Sleat—after a long and active life, most of which was passed in warfare—died, leaving no issue. He was succeeded by Donald Gorme Og Macdonald, son of his brother Archibald. Donald Gorme Og attended the court of King James in the summer of the following year, while his Majesty attended a meeting of parliament held in Edinburgh. On that occasion his Majesty knighted Sir Donald (Gorme Og) Macdonald, and some other barons, " with great solemnitie, in the palace of Holyrudhous." An action at law, between Sir Rory Mòr and the late Donald Gorme Mòr, as to some lands in Skye, was continued by Sir Donald Macdonald, " and about the yeir 1618 ther wes ane aggriement and arbitrall decreit past betuein them at Edinburgh, whereby a certane summ of money wes decerned to Sir Rorie for the clame of these lands, and that he should have possession of these lands for some yeirs to pay himselff. At the issue of the tyme prefixt by that decreit, the inheritance of that land should return to Sir Donald Mackonald, and to his heyrs." In 1625 Sir Rory Mòr and a body of his clan were engaged in suppressing the Clan Ian of Ardnamurchan. In course of the following year Sir Rory died, and was succeeded in the chieftainship by his son John. Whether we regard Sir Rory Macleod's great influence as a Highland chieftain, his military prowess and resources, or his princely hospitality, we cannot but see that he well entitled himself to the distinction of "Mòr" (great). It is not to be surprised that his piper, Patrick Mòr MacCrimmon, should have taken his death very much to heart. He could no longer wait at Dunvegan Castle, but, shouldering his great pipe, he made for his house at Borreraig, and composed, and struck up, as he went along, " Cumha Ruairidh Mhoir" (Rory Mòr's Lament), which is regarded to be the most melodious, feeling, and melancholy, *piobaireachd* known.   The Gaelic words to this air may be here given, with an English trans- lation :—

> *Tog orm mo phiob 'us theid mi dhaehaidh,*
> *'S duilich leam fhein, mo leir mar thachair ;*
> *Tog orm mo phiob 'us mi air mo chradh,*
> *Mu Ruairidh Mor, mu Ruairidh Mor.*
>
> *Tog orm mo phiob—tha mi sgith ;*
> *'S mur faigh mi i theid mi dhachaidh ;*
> *Tog orm mo phiob—tha mi sgith,*
> *'Smi air mo chradh mu Ruairidh Mor.*
>
> *Tog orm mo phiob—tha mi sgith,*
> *'S mur faigh mi i theid mi dhachaidh,*
> *Clarsach no piob cha tog mo chridh,*
> *Cha bheo fear mo ghraidh, Ruairidh Mor.*

> My pipe hand me and home I'll go,
> This sad event fills me with woe ;
> My pipe hand me, my heart is sore,
> My Rory Mòr, my Rory Mòr.
>
> My pipe hand me—I'm worn with woe,
> For if you don't then home I'll go ;
> My pipe hand me—I'm weary, sore,
> My heart is grieved for Rory Mòr.
>
> My pipe hand me—I'm worn with woe,
> For if you don't then home I'll go,
> Nor harp nor pipe shall cheer me more,
> For gone 's my friend, my Rory Mòr.

The following note, bearing on the hospitality of Sir Rory Mòr, is appended to one of the editions of Scott's " Lord of the Isles" :—" There is in the Seabhar Dearg a song intimating the overflowing gratitude of a bard of Clan Ronald, after the exuberance of a Hebridean festival at the patriarchal fortress of Macleod.   The translation being obviously very literal, has greatly flattered, as I am informed, the enthusiastic gratitude of the ancient bard ; and it must be owned that the works of Homer or Virgil, to say nothing of Mac- vuirich, might have suffered by their transfusion through such a medium.   It is pretty plain that when the tribute of poetical praise was bestowed, the horn of Rorie Mòre had not been inactive :"—

UPON SIR RODERIC MOR MACLEOD, BY NIALL MOR MACVUIRICH.

The six nights I remained in the Dunvegan, it was not a show of hospitality I met with there, but a plentiful feast in thy fair hall, among thy numerous host of heroes.

The family placed all around under the protection of their great chief, raised by his prosperity and respect for his warlike feats, now enjoying the company of his friends at the feast. Amidst the sound of harps, overflowing cups, and happy youth unaccustomed to guile or feud, partaking of the generous fare by a flaming fire.

Mighty Chief, liberal to all in your princely mansion filled with your numerous warlike host, whose generous wine would overcome the hardiest heroes, yet we continued to enjoy the feast, so happy our host, so generous our fare.

Sir Rory Mòr left five sons, who inherited his bravery, and his loyalty to the house of Stewart, viz. :—John Macleod of Dunvegan, Chief of the clan, Sir Roderick Macleod of Tallisker, Sir Norman Macleod of Bernera, William Macleod of Hamer, and Donald Macleod of Grishernish. Sir Rory's daughter, Janet, was married to John *Garbh MacGilliechallum* of Raasay, who served heir to that estate on 22d September 1648. Another daughter of Sir Rory's was married to Lachlean Maclean of Coll. John Macleod died in September 1649, leaving two sons, Roderick, the heir, then a minor, and John, and a daughter Sybella, who was married to Lord Thomas Fraser of Beaufort. Sir Roderick Macleod of Tallisker acted as guardian of his nephew, Roderick, during his minority, and raised a regiment of Macleods for the service of Charles II., of which Sir Norman Macleod was Lieutenant Colonel. Sir Roderick and Sir Norman were both present at the battle of Worcester, and are said to have received the honour of knighthood before the battle. Their piper, Patrick Mòr Maccrimmon, played in presence of the King on that occasion, and was allowed the honour of kissing the King's hand, on which he composed the air or *piobaireachd*, " *Thug mi pog do laimh an Righ*" (I gave a kiss to the King's hand). The Gaelic words to this air are :—

Thug mi pog 'us pog 'us pog,
Gun d' thug mi pog do laimh an Righ ;
'S cha d'chuir gaoth 'an craicionn caorach,
Fear a fhuair an fhaoilt ach mi.

The Macleods suffered severely at Worcester.   Sir Roderick made his escape, but Sir Norman was detained as prisoner for eighteen months.   They continued thereafter to render much assistance to the cause of the King.

Roderick Macleod, the minor, was called " Roderick the witty."   He married Margaret, daughter of Sir John Mackenzie of Tarbat, but dying without issue, he was succeeded in the estates and chieftainship by his brother John, known as John *Breac* Macleod.

CHAPTER XIII.

ON 14th July 1625, Sir Donald Gorme Og Macdonald of Sleat was created a Baronet of Nova Scotia, by Charles I., with a special clause of precedency, placing him second of that order in Scotland, Sir Robert Gordon, tutor of Sutherland, being the first baronet. The title has been described as " the true mean or honor between a baron of Parliament and a knight."   In November 1629 the King granted to these knights baronets " the privilege and libertie to weare about their necks a cheyne of gold, or ane orange tauny ribban, whereon shall hang pendant a salture azure in a scutcheon argent (that is, a blue Sanct Andrew's croce in a whyt feild), and thereon ane inscutcheon of the armes of Scotland, with ane imperiall croun above the scutcheon and incircled with this motto, *Fax mentis honestae gloria ;* whereby they shall be distinguished in all future aiges from all other orders."   Sir Donald adhered stedfastly to the cause of the King.   In 1640 he along with a number of other Scotch noblemen went to England to countenance and assist his Majesty, he having been called thither by three several letters from the King. For this alleged offence they were charged to appear before the Covenanting Parliament in Scotland, to answer as incendiaries and deserters of their country. Sir Donald died in 1643. He had been married to Janet, commonly called " fair Janet," second daughter of Kenneth, first Lord Mackenzie of Kintail. He was succeeded in the title and estates by his eldest son, Sir James Macdonald, called Sir James Mor. His second son, Donald Gorme Macdonald, possessed the lands of Castleton, in Sleat, from whom are descended the Macdonalds of Castleton.

In the year 1644, King Charles I. was compelled by the Covenanters to escape to Ireland. While there he was much assisted by the Earl of Antrim, a descendant of one of the Lords of the Isles. The Earl raised a body of troops and placed them under Alexander Macdonald, better known by the patronymic *Alastair Mac Cholla Chitich MhicGhilleasbuig,* with instructions to sail with them for Skye, where he was to give up the command to Sir Donald Macdonald, who was appointed by the King to be their General. On the arrival of the fleet at Loch Eisord, in Sleat, Alexander Macdonald learned that Sir Donald Macdonald was dead, and he offered the command to Sir James, who declined it, as the King's cause appeared to him to be desperate. Upon this Alexander resolved to return to Ireland with the men, but before he could leave the loch he was attacked by three men-of-war, sent thither from Leith by the Covenanting Parliament. The Covenanters gained the battle, and Alexander's own ship was taken. He was forced by this mishap to make his way with the remnant of his troops into Argyleshire, where he was joined by the chiefs of Clanranald and Glengarry, with their clansmen, and was able to afford material help to the Marquis of Montrose, who conducted the King's cause, and who, by the King's desire, raised Alexander to the rank of Major-General, and conferred on him the honour of knighthood. Macleod of Dunvegan, though urged by his friend the Captain of

K

Clanranald, refused to join Montrose. Sir James Macdonald of Sleat joined Montrose in 1645, and many of his clan fought under the Marquis at the battle of Inverlochy on 2d February of that year. Sir James sent a number of his clan to the assistance of Charles II. when he marched into England in 1651, many of whom took part in the battle of Worcester. Donald Macdonald of Kingsburgh, grandson of the warrior Donald MacIain Mhic Sheumais, was also a great loyalist, and was present with Montrose at all his battles. The Laird of Mackinnon also joined Montrose, and fought at the battle of Inverlochy. In 1650 Lachlan Mackinnon of Strath raised a regiment of his clan for the service of Charles II., and at the battle of Worcester he was made a knight banneret. In the Valuation Roll of the County of Inverness, dated 1644, the Laird of Mackinnon's rental, in the Parish of Kilchrist (Strath), is entered at £2400 Scots. The Laird of Macleod, designed "Sir John Macleod of Dunvegan," stood highest in the value of land in the county on that year. His rental in Skye amounted to £7000 Scots. The names of his four brothers also appear in that roll, viz. :—Parish of Kilbride, Norman Macleod, valued rent £533 6s 8d ; Kilmuir, William Macleod, £533 6s 8d ; Donald Macleod, £666 13s 4d ; and Oynert and Bracadale, Rorie Macleod, £1200. The Laird of Raasay's rental was £666 13s 4d. Raasay was then included in the parish of Snizort. Sir James Macdonald of Sleat stood the fourth highest as a landowner in the county. His rental in the parishes of Kilmure, Trotternish, Snizort, and Sleat in Skye, amounted to £6200. In 1663, Alexander *Macdhomhnuil Ghlas,* the young chief of Keppoch, and his brother, were assassinated by the daggers of some of their discontented clansmen. The Government, finding it impossible to bring the perpetrators of this cruel deed before a court of justice, sent a commission of fire and sword to Sir James Macdonald, signed by the Duke of Hamilton, Marquis of Montrose, Earl of Eglington, and others of the Privy Council, with authority to pursue, seize, and bring in, dead or alive, those lawless ruffians and their associates. This he expeditiously and effectually accomplished. Some of them he put to death, and disposed of the rest to the satisfaction of the whole Court, which contributed much to the peace of those parts. A letter, dated 15th December 1665, signed by the Earl of Rothes, was sent to Sir James, thanking him for his services, and assuring him that they would not be unrequited. Sir James's conduct on this occasion called forth an effusion from the great Jacobite bard, *Iain Lom*, who had in a previous composition, lamenting the death of the Keppoch chief and his brother, *Cumha clann na Ceapaich*, urged Sir James to avenge their death :—

Shir Sheumais nan tur 's nan baideal
Gheibh thus muirne cuirn a' t-aitreabh,
Ge do rinn thu 'n dusal cadail
'Seibhinn leam do dhusgadh madainn.

In the *Cumha* the following lines occur :—

Ach a Mhoirfhear Chlann Donuill
'Sfad do chomhnuidh measg Ghall,
Dh'fhag thu sinne n'nr breislich,
Nach do fhreasdail thu'n t-am ;
Nach do ghleidh thu na h-itean
Chaidh gun fhiosdhuit air chall ;
Tha sinn corrach as t-aogais
Mur choluinn sgaoilte gun cheann.

Gur h-iomadh oganach sgaiteach
Lubbhachlach sgiath chrom ;
Eadar drochaid Allt Eire
'S Rugha shleibhte na 'n toun ;
An ceannadh leat eiridh
Mu 'm bi do chraiceann lan tholl,
'Sa rachadh bras ann a d' eirig
Dheadh Shir Sheumais na'n long.

Sir James was quite a cavalier of the period. When at home his mansion was enlivened by the presence of a gay and noble company, bent on mirth and music. The bard above quoted from, in another song, gives an animated description of Sir James's spacious hall, lighted up at night with candles of the purest wax, while young ladies of dazzling beauty entertained the

company with melodious music, and when the time
for feasting began there was no stint of sparkling
uisgebeatha, fion Spainteach dearg 's beoir.   But it was on
the field that Sir James more distinguished himself—

> *Nuair a rachadh thu strith,*
> *Ann an armailt an Righ,*
> *Bhitheadh do dhiollaid air mil each gorm.*

Two of Sir James's sisters were married to distinguished though extreme Royalists—Mary to Sir Ewen
Cameron of Locheil, and Margaret to Æneas Macdonell of Glengarry, afterwards Lord Macdonald of
Aros, who died without issue.   Sir James Macdonald
was married to Margaret, only daughter of Sir Roderick
Mackenzie of Tarbet, by whom he had a family of two
sons and three daughters, viz., Donald, sometimes
styled *Breac,* who succeeded to the title and estates,
Somerled of Sartle ; Katherine, married to Sir Norman
Macleod of Berneray ; Florence, to John *Breac* Macleod
of Dunvegan ; and Mary, to Donald Macdonell of Glengarry.   Sir James died in 1678, and was succeeded by
his son, Sir Donald *Breac* Macdonald, who married
Lady Mary Douglas, second daughter of Robert, Earl
of Morton.   Sir Donald, like his father, was a Royalist.
   It appears that during the reign of Charles II. and
James VII., Episcopalian ministers were settled in Skye.
Of these Donald Nicolson and Alexander Nicolson were
ministers of St Mary's, or Kilmuir, in Troternish, and
John Mackinnon served the kirk of Eynort in Minginish,
and the chapel of Saint Assind in Bracadale.   On the
appointment of an Archdeacon of the Isles, in 1662, by
Charles II., the churches of Sleat, Strath, Snizort, and
Lyndale, were assigned to him as his " proper kirks."
In the following year steps were taken by the Scottish
Parliament for supplying the Western Isles with ministers having the " Yrish tounge" (Gaelic), the vacant
stipends of the Bishoprick of the Isles having been
appointed to be paid yearly to " six expectants" and " six
scholars," who were preparing for the office of minister.
In 1665 the Bishop's teinds of the lands held by Mac-

donald of Sleat, Macleod of Dunvegan, and Mackinnon
of Strath, amounted to £1750, and the tax thereon for
the relief of beneficed persons, to £94 10s Scots.   In
1694 the rent payable by Sir Donald Macdonald and
the Laird of Macleod, to the Bishop of the Isles and
Argyle, is entered in the Valuation Roll at £200 Scots.

It is alleged that Sir Donald Macdonald, to gratify
King James VII., embraced Popery for a short time,
and that several of the families of his clan followed his
example, but whether that is true or not, it is certain
that he assisted King James's cause when it was most
desperate.   Macaulay writes that " Macdonald of Sleat,
the most opulent and powerful of all the grandees who
laid claim to the lofty title of Lord of the Isles, arrived
at the head of 700 fighting men, from Skye "   The
number of Skyemen under Sir Donald Macdonald
appears to be over estimated by Macaulay.   In the
" Memoirs of the Lord Viscount Dundee," by an officer
of the army, published in 1714, it is stated that early in
June 1689, when Dundee was at Keppoch, to which he
had retired out of the way of the army under General
Mackay, and to await the further mustering of the clans,
" he was joined by the honourable Sir Donald of the
Isles, with five hundred men, who, by reason of an
indisposition was obliged to return home, but left his
son, young Sir Donald, with my Lord Dundee."   A
few days thereafter Sir Donald Macdonald (the younger)
and his men fought under Dundee at the battle of
Killiecrankie, and contributed much towards obtaining
the victory.   The Macdonalds occupied the extreme left
in the battle.   " The Highlanders threw away their
plaids, haversacks, and all other utensils, and marched
resolutely and deliberately in their shirts and doublets,
with their fusils, swords, targets, and pistols rea y,
down the hill on the enemy, and received Macka 's
third fire before they pierced his line, in which many of
the Highland army fell.   Then the Highlanders fired,
threw down their fusils, rushed in upon the enemy with
sword, target, and pistol, who did not maintain their

ground two minutes after the Highlanders were amongst them." Five cousins of Sir Donald Macdonald were slain in the battle of Killiecrankie. One of these was Alexander Macdonald of Kingsburgh, and it is probable that James Macdonald of Capstil was another. Of the latter Martin writes, that on the night of Killiecrankie, on which he was slain, his cows gave blood instead of milk, which circumstance his family and other neighbours concluded as a bad omen. After Dundee's death the Highland army became somewhat disorganised, as Irish officers sought the command. This led Sir Donald to retire to Skye with his men. In the following winter Major General Buchan, Lord Seaforth, Colonel Brown, and some other officers, were sent from Ireland by King James to Sir Donald Macdonald of Sleat ; and Buchan, by his commission, being eldest Major General, commanded the army, and desired each clan to give him one hundred men, promising with them to raise the Lowlands. After a conference of the chiefs, they gave him 1500 men, with whom he marched to Cromdale, where he was defeated by Sir Thomas Livingston. He thereafter formed a junction with Major General Cannin, but as they could make no head against the army of King William, they dispersed. General Cannin and his officers went to Sir Donald Macdonald's, and remained at his residence in Skye for about nine months, until, by the advice of King James, they made the best terms they could with the Government of King William, after which they sailed for France, and joined King James at St Germains. Sir Donald's residence in Sleat was set on fire by a party of King William's troops, who landed from a war ship. They were forced to re-embark, after a skirmish in which twenty of them were killed. These were buried at Dun-Flo.

CHAPTER XIV.

SIR DONALD MACDONALD of Sleat died in 1695. He left three sons :—Sir Donald Macdonald, who succeeded to the title and estates, James Macdonald of Oransay, and William Macdonald of Vallay. Sir Donald had from an early age distinguished himself as a soldier, and he was generally styled *Domhnull a Chogaidh, i.e.,* Donald of the wars, or warlike Donald. On the breaking out of the rebellion of 1715, in the interests of James (son of James VII.), styled the Chevalier de St George, Sir Donald was summoned by the Lord Advocate to appear at Edinburgh, to give bail for his allegiance to Government, and threatening him with a year's imprisonment and other penalties, in the event of failure. Sir Donald, however, disregarded the summons, and, with 700 of his clan, joined the camp of the Earl of Seaforth at Alness. They marched to Perth, where they joined the Earl of Mar. From thence the Highland army marched to Dunblane, in the neighbourhood of which they met the army of the Government, and they joined battle at Sheriffmuir, on Sunday, 13th November 1715. Sir Donald's battalion was commanded by his two brothers, James and William, and being sent out with the Earl Marischal's horse to drive away a party under the Duke of Argyle, who were reconnoitring on the heights, he may be said to have opened the battle. In the description of the battle of Sheriffmuir, by the poetess *Sileas Nigheau MhicRhaonuill,* she refers to Sir Donald and his brothers :—

> *Beir soraidh gu Domhnull o'n Dun,*
> *Gu h-Uilleam 's gu Seumas na 'n triuir,*
> *'Nuair chruinnicheas-uaislean*
> *Do d' chinneach mu n' cuairt dhuit*
> *Glac an t-urram a fhuair thu le cliu.*

On the rebellion being suppressed Sir Donald returned to Skye at the head of about a thousand men. He, however, offered no resistance to Government, but did not surrender, as he had no assurance of pardon. He retired to his property of North Uist, where he remained until a ship was procured, which conveyed him to France. He was forfeited for being implicated in the rebellion, but the forfeiture was soon removed, the estates being redeemed by his brother William, when tutor during the minority of Sir Alexander Macdonald.

In the year 1664, "Lachlan M'Fingon of Strathordaill" was served heir to his father, John Mackinnon, in the lands and barony of Strath, with the four marklands of Scalpay, together with the salmon fishings, mill, and the Kyleakin ferryboat. Lachlan was succeeded in the chieftainship and estates by his son Donald Mòr Mackinnon. His second son John Mackinnon was married to Ann, daughter of Donald Macdonald, chief of Clan Ranald. The next family in importance to that of the chief of the Mackinnons, was the Corriechatachin family, the first of whom was a son of Mackinnon of that Ilk, and the family are now claimants to the chieftainship. Lachlan Mackinnon was possessor of Corriechatachin in 1700. He was married to Margaret, daughter of John Macrae, Episcopalian minister in Dingwall, who wrote a history of the Macraes, and who died in 1704. At the battle of Sheriffmuir one hundred and fifty of the Mackinnons fought under Sir Donald Macdonald.

John Breac Macleod of Dunvegan has been called a "model Highland chieftain." He had an established bard, harper, piper, and jester at Dunvegan Castle, all liberally provided for. His harper was Roderick Morrison, the celebrated *Clarsair Dall,* a native of Lewis, who was a born gentleman, and lived on that footing in Macleod's family. "He was the last person of this country who possessed the talents of bard and harper, of poet and composer of music, in an eminent degree." Of Dunvegan Castle it was well sung then :—

> '*An bu lionmhor cruit is clar,*
> '*S iomadh bard a sheinneadh sgeul ;*
> *B' iomadh slige doll mun cuairt*
> '*S dana maith ga luaidh le cheil.*

Macleod began to repair and make additions to Dunvegan Castle, but did not live to finish his design.
Calculating, however, that he would finish the improvements, he caused a Latin inscription, composed by the
parish minister, to be engraved on a stone in the
building. The following English rendering of the
inscription is given in Mr Carruthers' Notes to Boswell's
Tour :—" John Macleod, lord of Dunvegan, Harris, and
Vaternish, &c., united in marriage to Flora Macdonald,
restored in the year of the vulgar era, 1686, his Tower
of Dunvegan, long the very ancient abode of his
ancestors, which had fallen utterly into decay."

> He who his old ancestral ruined halls
>   Delights to renovate and build secure,
> Should follow still where justice, godlike, calls,
>   And shun each glittering snare, each faithless lure.
> Virtue supreme the meanest hut can raise,
> And impious vice the loftiest towers debase.

Macleod died in 1693, and his death was much lamented. Elegies were composed on the occasion by the
Clarsair Dall, and by the bard *Ruaridh MacMhuirich,*
which gave graphic descriptions of the music, mirth,
amusements, and displays of hospitality, for which
Dunvegan Castle was celebrated during the lifetime of
the deceased chieftain. Mary Macleod, who has been
described as " the inimitable poetess of the Isles, and
the most original of all our poets," died in the same
year with her chieftain, at the advanced age of 105
years. She had nursed five lairds of the Macleods, and
two of the Mackenzies. She is said to have always
worn a tartan *tonnag,* fastened in front with a large
silver brooch. John Breac Macleod was succeeded by
his son, Roderick Macleod, who in 1694 married
Isabel, daughter of the Earl of Seaforth. He dispensed with his father's retinue at Dunvegan Castle,
and adopted the manners of an English gentleman.
Having died without issue, he was succeeded by his
brother, Norman Macleod, who, in September 1703,
married Anne Fraser, daughter of Hugh, tenth Lord
Lovat, by his wife Lady Emillia Murray, daughter of

John, Marquis of Athol.   In 1699 Thomas Lord Lovat
died at Dunvegan Castle, and a monument was erected
to his memory in the Church-yard of Kilmuir, in
Durinish, which bore the following inscription :—
" This pyramid was erected by Simon Lord Fraser of
Lovat in honour of Lord Thomas, his father, a peer of
Scotland, and chief of the great and ancient clan of the
Frasers.   Being attacked for his birth-right by the
family of Atholl, then in power and favor with King
William, yet, by the valour and fidelity of his clan, and
the asistance of the Campbells, the old friends and
allies of his family, he defended his birth-right with
such greatness and fermety of soul, and such valour and
activity, that he was an honour to his name, and a
good pattern to all brave chiefs of clans.   He died in
the month of May 1699, in the 63rd year of his age, in
Dunvegan, the house of the Laird of Macleod, whòsè
sister he had married: by whom he had the above
Simon Lord Fraser, and several other children.   And,
for the great love he bore to the family of Macleod, he
desired to be buried near his wife's relations, in the
place where two of her uncles lay.   And his son,
Lord Simon, to show to posterity his great affection for
his mother's kindred, the brave Macleods, chooses rather
to leave his father's bones with them, than carry them
to his own burial place near Lovat."   The monument,
which is of freestone, is still standing, but the white
marble tablet, containing the above inscription, fell
down, and was broken about twenty years ago.

A " Description of the Western Isles" was published
in 1699 by M. Martin, a Skye gentleman.   The following extracts from his account of Skye will be of
interest :—

The inhabitants of this Isle are generally well proportioned, and their
complexion for the most part black.   They are not obliged to art in
forming their bodies, for nature never fails to act her part bountifully to
them, and perhaps there is no part of the habitable globe where so few
bodily imperfections are to be seen, nor any children that go more early.

The ancient dress worn by the women, and which is yet worn by some
of the vulgar, called *Arisad,* is a white plad having a few small stripes

of black, blue, and red; it reached from the neck to the heels, and was tied before on the breast with a buckle of silver or brass, according to the quality of the person. The plad being pleated all round, was tied with a belt below the breast. The belt was of leather, and several pieces of silver intermixed with the leather like a chain. The lower end of the belt has a piece of plate about eight inches long, and three in breadth, curiously engraven, the end of which was adorned with fine stones or pieces of red coral. They wore sleeves of scarlet cloth, clos'd at the end as men's vests, with gold lace round 'em, having plate buttons set with fine stones. The head-dress was a fine kerchief of linen strait about the head, hanging down the back taperwise; a large lock of hair hangs down their cheeks above their breast, the lower end tied with a knot of ribbands.

There are two fairs of late held yearly at Portry, on the east side of Skie; the convenience of the harbour, which is in the middle of the Isle, made 'em chuse this for the fittest place. The first holds about the middle of June, the second about the beginning of September. The various products of this and the adjacent Isles and Continent are sold here, viz., horses, cows, sheep, goats, hides, skins, butter, cheese, fish, wool, &c.

There is a smith in the parish of Kilmartin who is reckoned a doctor for curing faintness of the spirits. This he performs in the following manner:—The patient being laid on the anvil with his face uppermost, the smith takes a big hammer in both his hands, and making his face all grimace, he approaches his patient, and then drawing his hammer from the ground as if he designed to hit him with his full strength on the forehead, he ends in a feint, else he would be sure to cure the patient of all diseases; but the smith, being accustomed to the performance, has a dexterity of managing his hammer with discretion, though at the same time he must do it so as to strike terror in the patient; and this they say has always the designed effect. The smith is famous for his pedigree, for it has been observed of a long time that there has been but one only child born in the family, and that always a son, and when he arrived at man's estate the father died presently after; the present smith makes up the thirteenth generation of that race of people, who are bred to be smiths, and all of them pretend to this cure.

Some of the inhabitants of the Harries sailing round the Isle of Skie, with a design to go to the opposite mainland, were strangely surprized with an apparition of two men hinging down by the ropes that secured the mast, but could not conjecture what it meant. They pursued the voyage, but the wind turned contrary and so forced them into Broadford, in the Isle of Skie, where they found Sir Donald Macdonald keeping a Sheriff Court; and two criminals receiving sentence of death there, the ropes and mast of that very boat were made use of to hang these criminals. This was told me by several who had this instance from the boat's crew.

Sir Donald Macdonald of Sleat was married to Mary, daughter of Donald *Gorme* Macdonald of Castleton, by whom he had one son and four daughters. This warrior died in 1718, and was succeeded by his son Sir Donald, who died unmarried in 1720, when the title reverted to

his uncle Sir James Macdonald of Oransay. Sir James
was first married to Margaret, daughter of John Macdonald of Castleton, by whom he had one son, John,
who died young. His second wife was Janet, daughter
of Alexander Macleod of Grishernish, by whom he had
one son and three daughters. Sir James died in 1723,
and was succeeded by his son, Sir Alexander Macdonald, then a minor. Sir Robert Douglas of Glen-
bervie, the author of the Peerage and Baronage of
Scotland, was married to Margaret Macdonald, the
second daughter of Sir James.

Norman Macleod of Dunvegan was succeeded by his
son Norman Macleod, who in 1731 married Janet Macdonald, daughter of Sir Donald Macdonald (*a Chogaidh*)
of Sleat.

CHAPTER XV.

ABOUT the beginning of the eighteenth century there
lived about two miles south of Portree a man of the
name of Macqueen, whose Christian name was *Aodh, i.e.,*
Eugene. In consideration not only of his physical
development, but also of his great mental capacity, he
received the distinction of *Mor,* and was known by the
name of *Aodh Mor Maccuinn.* The site of his house can
still be traced on the farm of Totadhaog (*i.e., the walls
of Aodh's house*). Aodh was a man of great common
sense, and soon became famed for the clear and just
views he adopted when any question of difficulty came
before him. He was frequently resorted to to arbitrate
between disputants, and when the proprietors, who
dispensed justice in those days, had any matter brought
before them in which they had a difficulty to decide,
they referred the cause to the decision of Aodh, and his
judgment was final. His decisions were very popular,
and several of them are related. On one occasion two
of Macleed of Macleod's tenants came before him with
a cause. One of them had owned a cow, which fell

over a precipice at the sea-shore, and a boat belonging to the other being moored at the foot of the rock, the cow fell into it, made a hole through it and was killed. The owner of the boat demanded damages, or the payment of the price of the boat from the owner of the cow; while the owner of the cow denied liability, and pled that if the boat had not been there his cow might have survived. Macleod had a difficulty in the case, and he referred them to Aodh to decide the point, and accompanied them to his residence. On a statement of the case being made to Aodh, he inquired whose property the cow was. "Mine," replied the owner with some hesitation, as he thought the decision was to be against him. "Whose was the boat?" asks Aodh. "Mine," replied the boatman exultingly. "And whose property is the rock?" "Macleod's," was the reply. "It appears to me," says Aodh, "that the accident would not have happened were it not for the rock, and I therefore decide that Macleod, as owner of the rock, should pay to the owners the price of the boat and of the cow." Macleod implemented the decision without murmuring, as he was much more able to pay the loss than the other litigants.

On another occasion two men were sitting fishing on a rock near Portree, on an uncommonly stormy day. One of them was carried off his seat by a large wave, and his companion was only able to reach him with the line attached to his fishing rod, the hook fixing in the drowning man's eye, by which means he was dragged on shore. He lost the use of his eye in consequence, and some time thereafter quarrelling with his preserver, he demanded damages for the loss of his eye, and brought his preserver to a court. The novel and unreasonable demand was referred to Aodh's judgment, and he promptly decided that when there would be a storm of equal severity with that on which the pursuer lost his eye, he (the pursuer) should go into the sea at the place where he was carried out by the wave, and if he succeeded in gaining the shore without assistance from any person, the defender would then have to pay him damages for being the means of his losing the eye. This silenced the pursuer, and he was only too happy to avoid recovering the damages.

Aodh was famed for his hospitality, but he had an unfortunate habit of accompanying his guests, when they left his house, for a short distance, and administering a sound thrashing to them at parting. On one occasion he had a guest who had heard of this practice, and who felt somewhat uneasy as to how he would pass the ordeal. He resolved that he would avoid giving his host the slightest chance of taking offence. When they had about finished dinner, Aodh took up a small piece of cake, and having buttered it, handed it to his guest, who politely took it, saying that as he had done justice so well to the dinner to satisfy himself, he would take that much to please his host. On his leaving, Aodh accompanied him a short distance, and was about parting peaceably from him, when the guest remarked that he was much surprised at his allowing him off without the customary salutation, or rather chastisement, he generally bestowed on his guests at parting. Aodh replied, "I never chastise gentlemen;" and explained that he knew when his guest took the bit of cake from him at dinner that he was well bred, that that bit of cake at the end of the dinner was his test, and that when his guests refused it from him, it shewed that they either disrespected him, or had taken too much already, and they therefore deserved some chastisement. Aodh's secret soon became generally known, and he continued thereafter to give good dinners to his guests without the customary *dessert*.

Some of Aodh's descendants are yet living in Skye, and are said to have inherited the good sense and respectability of their worthy ancestor.

About the same time lived Donald Macleod of Grishernish, a near relative of Macleod of Macleod. *Grishernish* was somewhat eccentric and easily imposed upon, while his valet *Rury* was an adept in the science of imposition, and played several tricks on his master. On one occasion *Grishernish* and his valet were travelling across the hill from Dunvegan to Grishernish. *Rury* carried his master's bag, which he knew contained a quantity of tobacco, and as he was fond of a *puff*, he was at his wits' end how to secure some of the *weed*. A bright idea occurred to him. He placed a needle in the point of his staff, and as his master was walking through the long heather in front of him, he stabbed him in the calf of the leg with the needle. Grishernish immediately halted and exclaimed, "Rury, I am stung by a snake ! what can be done for me ?" Rury expressed his great sorrow at the untoward event, and said that if tobacco were coiled round the leg, from the ankle to the knee, it would extract the poison of the serpent. Grishernish was gratified at the prescription, as the tobacco was so accessible, and taking it out of the bag made Rury coil it round the wounded leg. In a few minutes Grishernish said the cure was a success, and that the pain was gone. The tobacco was taken off the leg, and he requested Rury to bury it under the ground somewhere, in case it might poison the person who might find it, if it was merely thrown away. Rury did not want better sport, and he placed it in a place of security, from which he helped himself when he got an opportunity. One day two of Grishernish's horses were fighting, and they fell over a high precipice into the sea and were drowned. He was from home, and on his arrival his servants informed him of the loss of the horses, expecting that he would manifest his displeasure at the news, and blame them for being careless ; instead of that, however, the only answer he made on hearing the circumstance was " What a splash they must have made !" *Nach iad riun 'am plumb.* He was a famous swordsman, and on one occasion, when exercising with the heir of Macleod of Macleod, he took all the buttons out of his coat with the point of his sword without injuring the coat, and was proceeding to take the buttons out of young Macleod's shirt, when he was interfered with.

In an account of the Highland Clans, written about
the year 1725, the following notices occur of the chiefs
of Sleat and Dunvegan :—" The present Macdonald of
Slate is a boy, being son to James Macdonald of
Orinsay, second brother to the late Sir Donald. The
next principal man of that family is William Macdonald, present tutor of Slate, and youngest brother to
the said Sir Donald. The principal residence of that
family is the castle of Duntuilm, situated in the north
part of the Isle of Skye. They have also another place
of residence, adorned with stately edifices, pleasant
gardens, and other regular policies called Armodel, upon
the south coast of the said Isle." Macleod "is a
gentleman of the greatest estate of any of our Highland
clans. His principal residence is the strong castle of
Dunveggan, in the Isle of Skye, in which place the most
part of his numerous clan reside, of whom are a great
number of gentlemen of good account."

In the year 1724 the Presbyteries of Skye, Loch-
carron, Abertarff, and the Long Island, were erected,
and formed into the Synod of Glenelg. In 1726 a part
of the parish of Snizort was disjoined, and, with
Raasay and Rona, erected into the present parish of
Portree, of which Mr Hugh Macdonald was first
minister.

In a letter from Norman Macleod of Macleod to John
Forbes of Culloden, the brother of the Lord President,
dated at Dunvegan, 19th December 1732, the following
reference is made as to smuggling in Skye:—" I
won't repeat what I spoke to you last harvest, about
getting the custom-house of Hornwa brought to Glenelg; but I tell you that in spite of me a deal of brandy
is run over this Island and neighbourhood, which I
assure you vexes me ; and to show my good inclination
for the quick sale of Ferintosh, procure in the meantime (which I'm informed can be got) a warrant from
the Commissioners of the Customs to me, and whom I
appoint, to seize vessels with counterband goods anie
where about Sky or Glenelg; and I'll warrant you ane

effectual stop shall be putt to that mischievous trade ; and wout it, I can do little." A contest for the representation of the County appears to have taken place in the same year, and several letters relating thereto are published in the Culloden Papers. In one of these the crafty Simon, Lord Lovat, thus lauds Macleod of Macleod to the Laird of Culloden :—" My cusin, the Laird of Macleod, is mighty kind in his letter to me ; it is most certainly to you yt. I owe his good intentions to serve me, and live in great fr'dship wt. me, but he desires yt. nobody but you and your brother should know it ; otherwise yt. it will put him out of condition to serve me, because of the weakness and jealousies of those he has to do with. Macleod is really a sweet-blooded young fellow, and has good sense and writs pretiely. I wish wt. all my soul yt. this great affair were ended, yt. we might live in an affectionat and strict fr'dship together—since I am ye nearest relation he has of his father and mother's kindreds."

CHAPTER XVI.

Sir Alexander Macdonald of Sleat was first married to Ann, daughter of David Erskine, Lord Dun, and dowager of James, Earl of Airlie. She died in about a year after marriage, leaving a son Donald, who died young. Her death took place in the absence of Sir Alexander in London, and on his arrival at home he was in great griet to find only her *remains* before him. On that occasion John Mackay *(Piobaire Dall)*, the Gairloch bard and piper, who used to be a frequent attendant on Sir Alexander, composed a song to him, consoling him on his bereavement. It is published in " Mackenzie's Beauties of Gaelic Poetry."

Sir Alexander afterwards married Lady Margaret Montgomery, daughter of Alexander, ninth Earl of Eglinton. Lady Margaret was exceedingly handsome, beautiful, and accomplished, which graces she, to a

M

great extent, inherited from her mother, the celebrated countess Susan, who was said to be the greatest
beauty of her day in Scotland. "Countess Susan's
daughters were all equally remarkable with herself for
a good mien; and *the Eglintonne air* was a common
phrase in their time. It was a goodly sight, a century
ago, to see the long procession of sedans, containing
Lady Eglintoune and her daughters, devolve from the
Close (Old Stamp Office Close, High Street), and proceed to the Assembly Rooms in the West Bow, where
there was usually a considerable crowd of plebeian
admirers, congregated to behold their lofty and graceful figures step from the chairs on the pavement. It
could not fail to be a remarkable sight,—eight beautiful women, conspicuous for their stature and carriage, all
dressed in the splendid though formal fashions of that
period, and inspired at once with dignity of birth and
consciousness of beauty."—(Traditions of Edinburgh.)
Even in her eighty-fifth year, Johnson said, the Countess had "little reason to accuse time of depredations on
her beauty," and Boswell describes her figure as
"majestic, her manners high-bred, her reading extensive, and her conversation elegant." Hamilton of
Bangour pays herself and her daughters a compliment
in the following lines :—

> Supremely blest by Heaven, Heaven's richest grace
> Confest is thine, an early blooming race ;
> Whose pleasing smiles shall guardian wisdom arm,—
> Divine instruction ! taught of thee to charm,
> What transports shall they to thy soul impart,
> (The conscious transports of a parent's heart),
> When thou behold'st them of each grace possesst,
> And sighing youths imploring to be blest !
> After thy image formed, with charms like thine,
> Or in the visit or the dance to shine :
> Thrice happy who succeed their mother's praise,
> The lovely Eglintounes of other days !

Lady Margaret was educated in a boarding-school near
London. She was a frequent guest in the house of
the Duchess of Buccleugh and Monmouth while there.
Her Grace maintained Royal state in her establishment,

" having only one seat in her rooms (and that generally under a canopy) for herself, so her visitors were compelled to stand:" but as Lady Margaret was a near relative of her Grace she." was allowed the extraordinary privilege of a chair." Lady Margaret is referred to in the ballad :—

> What charms can English Margaret boast
> To fix thy inconstant mind,
> And keep the heart that I have lost ?
> Oh cruel and unkind !
>
> For I can kilt my *coat* as high,
> And curl my *red toupee*,
> And I'll put on an *English mutch*,
> If that has charms for thee.

Lady Margaret took a kind and active interest in the welfare of the tenants on the Macdonald estates, which made her deservedly popular. " Mrs Mackinnon (of Corry) added that Lady Margaret was quite adored in Sky. That when she travelled through the island, the people ran in crowds before her and took the stones off the road, lest her horse should stumble and she be hurt."—(Boswell's Tour.) Sir Alexander himself was also popular, and his hospitality was unbounded. A hogshead of claret was said to be the weekly consumption of his table. He made Skye his constant residence, and maintained a popular influence over his clan.

Considerable alarm and excitement occurred in Skye and Harris in the year 1739, on account of several persons, of both sexes, having been kidnapped and taken on board a large ship, which had put in to several places on the coast, and sailed away with them, bound for the Southern States of America, where, it was said, they were to be sold as slaves. The ship was wrecked on the north coast of Ireland, and the passengers were fortunately saved. Many of them settled there, and a few were able, with difficulty, to find their way back to their island homes. The leader of this band of kidnappers was Norman Macleod, a young man, and son of Donald Macleod, tacksman of Berneray. Norman made his escape in Ireland, and remained for some time in concealment, but on the breaking out of the rebellion of 1745, he appeared in public, joined the Government army, was captain of one of the independent companies raised by Macleod of Macleod, and exerted himself zealously against the Jacobites, of which his father was a keen partisan. As Donald Macleod had distinguished himself in the cause of the Prince, there was a strict search made for him after the rebellion, in which his son Norman took an active part. He, however, eluded the search, and after the act of indemnity lived to a ripe old age, at his house of Berneray. His tomb in the burying-ground of St Clements, Harris, bears the following quaint inscription :—

" To the memory of Donald Macleod of Berneray, son of John, Tutor of Macleod, who, in vigour of body and mind, and firm adherence to the principles of his ancestors, resembled the men of former times. His grandfather and granduncle were knighted by King Charles II., for their loyalty and distinguished valour in the battle of Worcester. When the standard of the House of Stuart, to which he was attached, was displayed in 1745, tho' passed the prime of life, he took arms, had a share in the actions of the period, and in the battle of Falkirk vanquished a dragoon hand to hand. From that time he lived at his house of Berneray, universally beloved and respected. In his 75th year he married his third wife, by whom he had nine children,* and died in his 90th year, the 16th December 1783. This monument was erected by his son Alexander Macleod of Herris, Esq."

Norman Macleod succeeded his father as tacksman of Berneray. He was much respected in his latter days. He introduced many improvements into the island, manufactured kelp extensively, was a large holder of stock, and was reckoned the first tacksman in the Western Isles in his day. His daughter, Ann, was married to Captain Norman Macleod of Peninduin, Skye, who died in May 1804, and was by him the mother of the late William Macleod of Orbost, Lieutenant Roderick Macleod, killed at the siege of San Sebastian,

---

* Donald of Bernerary by his third marriage had three sons and six daughters, and by the death of his grandson, Donald J. Macleod, Major in the Scots Greys, who died in 1852, only son of Lieutenant-General Sir John Macleod, the Berneray branch in the direct male line became extinct.—*Inverness Courier, 4th February* 1869.

and Donald Macleod, Inspector-General of Hospitals, Bengal, who died at Calcutta, 12th November 1840.

In his old age, Norman of Berneray resented the slightest reference to *Soitheach nan Daoine*, as the would-be slave ship was termed. The following letter, from Lady Margaret Macdonald to Lord Justice-Clerk Milton, relative to this affair of the kidnapping, appears in the Culloden Papers :—

SKY, Jany. 1, 1740.

DEAR JUSTICE,—Being informed by different hands from Edr. that there is a currant Report of a Ship's haveing gon from thiss Country with a greate many people disignd for America, and that Sir Alexr. is thought to [have] concurred in forceing these people away. As I am positive of the falsehood of this, and quite acquainted with the danger of a Report of this kind, I begg leave to informe Your Lodp. of the reall matter of fact. In Hervest last wee were pritty much alarmed with accounts from different Corners of thiss and some neighbouring Islands, of persons being seized and carry'd aboard of a Ship which putt into differant places on thiss coast. Sir Alexr. was both angery and Concern'd at that time to hear that some of his oune people were taken in this manner ; but cou'd not learn who were the Actors in thiss Wicked scrape till the Ship was gon. One Normand M'Leod, with a number of Fellows that he had pick'd up to execute his intentions, were the Real Actors of thiss affair. Sir Alexr. never made much noise about the thing in hop's that thiss Normd. M'Leod might some time or other cast up ; But he has never Yet appaired in thiss part of the World, and probably never will, as the thing has made so much noise ; he's accomplices have betaken themselves to the Hills, and lately rob'd a Servt. of ours comeing from Edr. out of pique to his master ; and one of them knock'd him doun and cutt him over the head terribly. Sir Alexr. is just now bussy indeavouring to detect any of these Rogues that may be Yet in Sky, and hopes soon to apprehend some of those who have left it. Tho' thiss is the real matter of fact Sir Alexr. can't help being concerned that he shou'd be any ways mentioned in the story, tho' quite inosent. This affair has made so much noise with You because of the way it has been represented from Irland that possibly there may be an intention of prosecuting Sir Alexr. If that shou'd go on, tho' it cannot be dangerouse to him, Yett it cannot faill of being both troublesome and expensive ; And therefore lett me begg of Your Lorp. to write to the people of poure above to prevent thiss impending Evell, because a little time may bring the real Actors to a tryall, which I dare say Your Lorp. wou'd rather see in a pannel than imagenary persones that had no hand in the matter. Tho' I have no reasone to believe Your Lorp. will bo remiss in any affair of such consiquence to us both, my anxiety obligess me to intreate You'll take this affair so much into consideration that You'll delay no time in makeing applications where You judge it proper ; and trust me Dr. Justice, thiss favour shall make me with more gratitude than ever, Your most Obdt. and ever devoted Servt.,

(Signed) MARGTT. MACDONALD.

In 1731 a secret association for promoting the interests of the Chevalier de St George existed in Scotland. James Erskine of Grange, brother of the Earl of Mar, and a Lord of Session by the designation of Lord Grange, was connected with this association, and his wife, Lady Grange (daughter of Chiesly of Dalry), a beautiful woman, but of a most violent and irregular temper, having accidentally obtained possession of papers intended for her husband, she became aware of the designs of the association. She remonstrated with her husband, but as he paid no attention to her, she threatened to reveal the plots of the society to Government. Lord Grange became alarmed, and informed his Jacobite friends, who resolved with his approval to have the lady secured and carried away to some unfrequented and safe place. Lord Grange attempted to justify this proceeding by giving it the legal term of *sequestrating his wife* as a person of unsound mind, and unfit to have the management of her family. Simon, Lord Lovat, was the moving spirit in the plot, and it is alleged that Sir Alexander Macdonald and Norman Macleod of Macleod gave it countenance. The conducting of the cruel transaction was entrusted to Macdonald of Morar, and to John Macleod, advocate, a relative of Macleod of Macleod. Lady Grange was seized in her lodging in Edinburgh at midnight of the 22d January 1732, a cloth was tied over her face to prevent her from seeing where she was going or calling for assistance, and having been placed on horseback she was led away at dead of night. After a fatiguing and dangerous journey across one of the wildest districts of Scotland, she was detained a prisoner in Castle Tyrim until removed to the remote island of Heiskar, on the west coast of North Uist, then belonging to Sir Alexander Macdonald, where she was kept for nearly two years. From thence she was removed to St Kilda, where she was detained for seven years, debarred from holding any communication even by letter with her friends. After ten years of banishment she at length managed to send a note to her friends, concealed in a ball of yarn. Steps were then taken to rescue her, but before they could be successful, she was removed from St Kilda to Assynt, and from thence to Skye, where it was said she was for some time kept in a cave, but her persecutors finding it too troublesome to attend her there, allowed her to leave it and go where she pleased. By that time her reason had given way, and she wandered over Skye in a state of idiocy, supported by the charity of the people, until at length she was overcome with misery and disease, and closed her chequered life at Idrigal, in Waternish, in the month of May 1745. She was secretly buried in the church-yard of Trumpan.

In 1741 there was a keen contest for the representation of the County of Inverness, between Normand Macleod of Macleod, and Sir James Grant of Grant, in which Macleod was successful. Sir Alexander Macdonald would not qualify as a voter, and remained neutral during the contest. Much pressure was brought to bear by both sides on John Mackinnon of Mackinnon, who was at the time in straitened circumstances, but he voted for Macleod, who was then very popular, and acknowleged to be a man of culture and talent. His grandson (General Macleod) wrote of him:—"With a body singularly well made and active he possessed very lively parts. The circumstances of the times introduced him to the public with great advantage; and, until the unfortunate 1745, he was much considered. His independent fortune, and promising character, early obtained him the representation in Parliament of Inverness-shire, his native county. The numbers and fidelity of his clan, and his influence with his neighbours, were known; and I have reason to believe that many allurements were held out to seduce him into engagements which were then considered only as dangerous, but neither guilty nor dishonourable."

CHAPTER XVII.

The news frae Moydart cam yestreen,
Will soon gar mony ferlie,
That ships o' war hae just come in,
And landed royal Charlie.

HISTORY has few such surprising and romantic chapters as the event of the *Forty-five.* On the 23d day of July 1745, Prince Charles Edward Stewart, the young Chevalier, arrived in the French frigate Doutelle, in the sound of Barra, and landed in the Island of Eriskay, attended only by seven gentlemen who had accompanied him from France. On the spot where he landed, which is a sandy knoll called *Coileag-a-Phrionnsa, i.e.,* the Prince's knoll, Charles planted a convolvulus, which still flourishes on that exposed and rugged island, and which the natives call *Flur a Phrionnsa, i.e.,* the Prince's flower. The Prince was conducted to the house of Angus Macdonald, the tacksman of the island. He was there made aware that Ranald Macdonald (young Clanranald) was at Moydart on the mainland, and that Ranald Macdonald, the old chief of Clanranald, was in the adjoining island of South Uist, with his brother, Alexander Macdonald of Boisdale. As Clanranald was the chief of a numerous and powerful branch of the Macdonalds, who had hitherto been firm supporters of the cause of the Stuarts, it was necessary for the Prince, in his present undertaking, to secure his support, and the services of his clan ; and he accordingly sent a messenger to Macdonald of Boisdale, desiring an interview, Boisdale being a man of superior talents and sagacity, and supposed to have great influence over his brother and nephew of Clanranald. Boisdale obeyed the summons, and came on board the Doutelle next morning. Though well affected towards the Prince's cause, he was impressed with its hopelessness without foreign assistance, and after the Prince had made his proposals, Boisdale plainly advised him to return home.

The Prince replied he had come *home*, and that he had every confidence in his Highlanders, instancing Sir Alexander Macdonald of Sleat, and the Laird of Macleod (who could bring upwards of 2000 men to the field). Boisdale gave him the unwelcome assurance that these chiefs would not adhere to his interest, but that they would probably act against him. " He added withal, that if Sir Alexander Macdonald and the Laird of Macleod declared for him, it was his opinion he might then land on the continent, for he doubted not but he would succeed in the attempt; but if they happened to refuse their assistance (which he still insisted would be the case), then their example would prove of bad consequence, and would tend only to make others backward, and to keep at home; and in that event he still thought it advisable to suggest his returning back to where he came from."—(Jacobite Memoirs, p. 12.) Charles was taken aback by Boisdale's apparent coldness, and exerted his eloquence to make him relent, which, however, proved vain. Boisdale recommended the Prince to send a messenger to Sir Alexander Macdonald to test what he had said, and accordingly the Prince did send a message to Sir Alexander, intimating his arrival, and demanding assistance. Without waiting for the return of the messenger, Charles advanced in his frigate towards the mainland, and on the following day cast anchor in the bay of Lochnanuagh, between Moydart and Arisaig. Boisdale was likely to have been well informed as to the state of politics in Skye at the time, as he was connected with Skye by marriage, his wife being Margaret Macdonald, daughter of John Macdonald of Castleton, Sleat, and step-mother of Sir Alexander Macdonald, she having been the second wife and widow of Sir James Macdonald of Orinsay.

At Lochnanuagh the Prince was waited upon by young Clanranald, who was much of his uncle's way of thinking, as to the improbability of success in the undertaking. A long interview resulted in young Clanranald and Allan Macdonald, brother of Kinloch-

moydart, being deputed to go to Skye and request Sir
Alexander Macdonald and Macleod of Macleod—whom
the Prince still considered faithful to him—to join him
at once with their forces. The envoys found both chiefs
at Dunvegan Castle. Sir Alexander replied to the
Prince's message that he considered the enterprise at
that time desperate, and that as he had not given an
explicit promise to join the Prince, he was resolved not
to do so. Macleod excused himself by stating that his
agreement with the Prince depended on his bringing
auxiliaries from abroad, and that as a large number of
his clansmen resided in the outer islands, it would take
considerable time to assemble them. They even shook
young Clanranald in his resolution to join the Prince,
and he left Skye with the purpose of importuning him
to return to France. On reporting his unsuccessful
mission, the Prince was advised to give up the enterprise, as the example of the Skye chiefs would be sure
to be imitated by others. Charles, however, would not
relinquish his purpose, and his undaunted and hopeful
spirit inspired those who came in contact with him with
enthusiasm in his cause. Clanranald was again enlisted
in the Prince's cause, and he at once set about raising
his clansmen on the mainland. Immediately on Clanranald's visit to the Skye chiefs, Macleod of Macleod
wrote Duncan Forbes of Culloden, the Lord President
of the Court of Session, the following letter, which was
the first information the Government received of the
Prince's arrival :—

My Dearest Lord,—To my no small surprise, it is certain that the
Pretended Prince of Wales is come on the coast of South Uist and Barra,
and has since been hovering on parts of the coast of the main land that
lies betwixt the point of Ardnamurchan and Glenelg ; he has but one
ship, of which he is aboard ; she mounts about 16 or 18 guns. He has
about thirty Irish or French officers with him, and one Sheridan, who is
called his Governor. The Duke of Athol's brother is the only man of
any sort of note (that once belonged to this country) that I can hear of
that's alongst with him. His view I need not tell you was to raise all
the Highlands to assist him, &c. Sir Alex. Macdonald and I not only
gave no sort of countenance to these people, but we used all the interest
we had with our neighbours to follow the same prudent method ; and I
am persuaded we have done it with that success, that not one man of any

consequence benorth the Grampians will give any sort of assistance to this mad rebellious attempt. How far you think we acted properly, I shall long to know ; but this is certain, we did it as our duty and for the best, for, in the present situation of Affairs in Europe, I should have been sorry to see anything like disaffection to the Government appear, tho' ever so trivial, or that there was occasion to march a single company to quell it, which now I hope and daresay is not.

As it can be of no use to the public to know whence you have this information, it is, I fancy, needless to mention either of us ; but this we leave in your own breast, as you are a much better judge of what is, or is not, proper to be done. I've wrote to none other, and as our friendship and confidence in you is without reserve, so we doubt not of your supplying our deffects properly. Sir Alex. is here, and has seen this scrawl.—I ever am, most faithfully, yours,

DUNVEGAN, 3d *August* 1745.   NORMAND MACLEOD.

    THE LORD PRESIDENT, &c.

P.S.—Last night I had the pleasure of yours of the 25th. A thousand thanks for your advice, but I'm in good health by the very means you mention, moderate exercise and regularity without starving. Young Clanranald has been here with us, and has given us all possible assurance of his prudence, &c.*

Sir Alexander Macdonald wrote the Lord President on the 11th of August, from Tallisker, where he was on a visit, assuring his Lordship of his own and Macleod's loyalty to the Government, as also that of Hector Maclean, laird of Coll, who was visiting his son-in-law at Tallisker at the same time. Maclean of Coll, though not the chief, had the principal direction of the Clan Lean at this period, but he was not able to deter a large number of the clan joining the Prince, under the leadership of Maclean of Drimmin, who afterwards fell at Culloden. Coll's daughter, Mary, was married to Colonel John Macleod of Tallisker. There were several intermarriages between the families of Coll and Tallisker. Isabella, daughter of Sir Roderick Macleod of Tallisker, was the mother of Hector Maclean, 11th laird of Coll, before mentioned ; Florence, daughter of Lachlan Maclean, 8th of Coll, was married to John Macleod of Tallisker, father of the Colonel, and her sister Catherine to his cousin, Norman Macleod of Grishernish ; Janet, the eldest daughter of the last-

---

* Culloden Papers, p. 203.

mentioned Tallisker, was married to Hugh Maclean, 13th of Coll, whose grand-daughter Catherine, was married to Major Donald Macleod of Tallisker.

On the 19th August 1745, the Lord President acknowledged Sir Alexander Macdonald's letter from Tallisker, stating that his own and Macleod's conduct and resolution gave him " very great satisfaction," and that he was "heartily glad to hear of the wise resolution" of his friend Coll. On the 17th August, Macleod of Macleod wrote the Lord President a letter dated at *Sconser*, in which he mentioned that Sir Alexander and he could " easily raise from 1500 to 2000 men for the King's service," but that they would require arms. On the 20th August, the Prince unfurled his father's standard at Glenfinnon, surrounded by about 800 of the Cameron men. Macdonald of Keppoch arrived in about an hour thereafter with 300 of his clan, and in course of the same day some gentlemen of the name of Macleod arrived and offered their services. They professed to be indignant at the conduct of their chief, and proposed to return to Skye and raise as many men of the clan as they could, Macleod of Swordland engaging to take the fort of Bernera in Glenelg, and to bring a hundred men to the assistance of Charles, an engagement he was not able to perform.

After his success at the battle of Prestonpans (or Gladsmuir), Prince Charles on the 24th day of September despatched one of his *aides-de-camp*, Alexander Macleod of Muiravonside, advocate (great-grandson of Sir Norman Macleod of Bernera, and a cousin of young Clanranald), to Skye, to induce Sir Alexander Macdonald and Macleod of Macleod to repair at once with their clansmen to him at Edinburgh, where they would be well received and furnished with arms, and that he would not impute their delay in hitherto joining him to disloyalty to his father's cause, but to the private manner in which he came to Scotland. Sir Alexander Macdonald again refused to join the Prince. The arguments and solicitations of his kinsman appear to have made Macleod of Macleod waver as to what course he should take, and while visiting Lord Lovat at Castle Downie, he engaged to meet the Frasers at Corryarrack, on the 15th day of October, with his men, and join the Prince's army with them, but on returning to Skye and consulting with Sir Alexander Macdonald, he resolved to stay at home. Alexander Macleod was also desired to send for Mackinnon of Strath, and to tell him that the Prince was surprised that he should have failed in his solemn promise to join him with his men. Mackinnon, however, appears to have been on the march south, with one hundred and twenty of his followers, by this time, and joining the Prince in the neighbourhood of Edinburgh on the 13th day of October, he accompanied the army on the march into England. Malcolm Macleod (the MacGillechallum) of Raasay, with his third son, Murdoch (Dr Murdoch Macleod of Eyre), and his nephew, Captain Malcolm Macleod, also joined the Prince with one hundred of the Siol Torquil, or Macleods of Raasay. In the Account of Charge and Discharge by Mr Murray of Broughton, secretary to the Prince, published in the appendix to Chambers's History of the Rebellion, there are the following entries of sums advanced to Mackinnon of Strath and Macleod of Raasay :—

3 and 4. This gentleman is still alive, and Mr M. is ready to believe is a person of veracity and will acknowledge it.

> 3. To the Laird of Mackinnon, the same day and place (at Callich, upon the side of Locharkik, where it was proposed to raise a body of men to continue the war) £40 0 0
>
> 4. Sent by do. to Macleod of Raza and Macdonald yr. of Scotus, being all that remained of the sum Mr M. then had carried with him 20 0 0

6 and 7. Mr Macleod, your. of Neuck, may remember this. Raza having wrote with a little too much warmth, Mr Macleod made an apology to Mr M. for him, and beg'd that it might not prevent him from sending a supply, and he will likewise remember that it was by his uncle Bernera that it was sent, and that Mr M. told him that he had given that gentleman £50. Mr M. is informed that Bernera is still alive.

6. Sent from the wood on the side of Locharkik by
   Macleod of Bernera to Macleod of Raza, upon
   receipt of a letter from him complaining that the
   former sum was too small £40 0 0
7. To Macleod of Bernera at the same time   ...   50 0 0

Macleod, younger of Neuck, appears to be the same
person with Alexander Macleod of Muiravonside, the
Prince's envoy to Skye, who was a cousin of Berneray's.
Donald Macleod of Berneray was also related to Macleod of Raasay, whose mother was Catherine, daughter
of Sir Norman Macleod of Berneray.   Raasay's
daughter Janet was married to John Mackinnon of
Strath ; another daughter, Flora, was married to Archibald Macqueen of Totterome, lieutenant of the company
of militia of which Hugh Macdonald of Armadale was
captain.   Raasay's eldest son and heir, John, did not
go out in the Rebellion, and his second son, Norman,
was an officer in the service of the States General.

CHAPTER XVIII.

EARLY in September the Ministry sent twenty commissions to the Lord President, for raising as many
independent companies of one hundred each in the
Highlands for the service of the Government.   He
instantly applied to Sir Alexander Macdonald and
Macleod of Macleod to raise companies of their clans,
but from the delay in procuring arms and money it
took two or three months before the Skye companies
mustered.   On the 24th day of September Sir Alexander wrote the President from Mugstot, that it was
quite impossible to raise the men without money unless
it was to follow himself.   On the 23d day of October,
Macleod of Macleod writes him from Dunvegan :—

There never was such dismal weather seen as we have had constantly
here ; hardly a day that it's possible to stir in any sort of business.
However, by the end of next week, Talisker, who has just got a son,
will be ready to move, and I will by that time have a body of 300 men
so disposed here that they can move on a day's notice. Sir Alexr. has

sent to Uist for his captain, and I am very hopeful he will be ready as soon as Talisker, or very quickly after. The behaviour of my son's men vexes me to the soul ; they were entertained in an outhouse of Lovat's and sent to the master's rendevous. Sandy Macleod is still here, waiting to see his uncle from Harris ; he has made some attempts to raise rebellion against the knight and me here, but with very bad success.

On the 24th October the President wrote Sir Alexander, stating the necessity of either he or Macleod marching at once to Inverness with a large body of men, while one of them should remain. in Skye " to give the people directions, and to keep the proper countenance in that country." The clan feeling in Skye was so high, that though the people were favourably disposed towards the Prince, yet they joined their chiefs to fight for the Government ; but it is alleged that many of them were not made aware when being enrolled whether they were to fight for King George or the Prince, and that they were disappointed when they found, on arriving in the Low Country, that they were required to fight for the Government against their brother Highlanders and Islesmen. There were, however, a few examples where the clan feeling did not prevail. Donald Macleod of Berneray, on being required to attend at Dunvegan with his *quota* of men, wrote his chief :—" I place at your disposal the twenty men of your tribe who are under my immediate command, and in any other quarrel would not fail to be at their head, but in the present I must go where a higher and more imperious duty calls me." Donald Roy Macdonald of Knockow, in Skye (a grandson of Sir James Mòr Macdonald of Sleat, and a brother of Hugh Macdonald of Baleshare, Sir Alexander's factor in North Uist), joined the Prince. He arrived in Edinburgh with the Mackinnons of Strath, and entered as a volunteer in Keppoch's regiment, who gave him a lieutenant's pay. " After the battle of Falkirk, young Clanranald took a liking for Donald Roy Macdonald, and made him a captain in his own regiment." Capt. Roy Macdonald, and James Macdonald, son of John Macdonald, tenant of the Island of Heisker, North

Uist, were the only gentlemen of Sir Alexander's following who joined the Prince. This James Macdonald was the great grandfather of the late Donald Macdonald, Esquire of Skeabost, Bernisdale, Edinbain, and Stein, in Skye. On the 15th day of November, four companies of the followers of Macleod of Macleod mustered at Inverness, and their officers then received their commissions. The officers were—Captains John Macleod younger of Macleod, Norman Macleod of Waterstein, Norman Macleod of Berneray, and Donald Macdonald; Lieutenants Alexander Macleod, Donald Macleod, John Campbell, and William Macleod; Ensigns John Macaskill, John Macleod, John Macleod, and Donald Macleod. These four companies and a company of one hundred men of the Macleods of Assynt, raised by Captain Macleod of Geanies, were commanded by Norman Macleod of Macleod, and on the 10th day of December he marched with them from Inverness, having been despatched towards Elgin to check Lord Lewis Gordon's recruiting and exactions in the shires of Banff and Aberdeen. At Elgin, Macleod of Macleod got information that a party of two hundred of the insurgents had taken possession of the passage of the Spey at Fochabers, which they intended to dispute with him, but on his advancing they retired, and he crossed the Spey unmolested. He then marched to Cullen, Banff, and Inverury. On the 23d day of December, they were nearly surprised at Inverury after nightfall by a superior force under Lord Lewis Gordon. Macleod had barely time to put his men under arms, and seize some posts of advantage in the town. He made a short stand, but his shot being expended he had to make a hasty retreat. The Macleods lost about forty men in the skirmish, but most of these were taken prisoners, very few being killed on either side. They recrossed the Spey and fled as far. as Elgin and Forres, when some of them left for home, not being zealous in the cause they were called to fight for. Macleod was again able to muster the most of his men, and he remained at Forres until, upon the news of the Prince's march from Stirling, he was called in to Inverness, where, on the 31st day of December, he was joined by two hundred of Sir Alexander Macdonald's men. These two companies were officered by Captain James Macdonald of Aird, Troternish, and Captain John Macdonald of Kirkibost, North Uist; Lieutenants Allan Macdonald of Knock, and Allan Macdonald (probably Allan Macdonald younger of Kingsburgh); and Ensigns James Macdonald and Donald Macdonald. Captains James Macdonald and John Macdonald were sons of William Macdonald the tutor, and therefore cousins of Sir Alexander Macdonald.

On the 16th February 1746, Prince Charles, with a small retinue, arrived at Moy Hall, the seat of the Mackintosh, whose lady had raised the clan for the Prince, though the laird himself was a partisan of the Government. The Earl of Loudon, who was at Inverness with near two thousand men, resolved to secure the Prince as prisoner, before he could be joined by his army, which was marching from the south. The Earl advanced towards Moy with 1500 men, the advance gua of 70 men being commanded by Macleod of Macleod Lady Mackintosh received private information of the contemplated attack, and sent the Prince to a place of safety. In the meantime she sent out a patrolling party of five men, armed with muskets, to watch the road from Inverness—of whom the blacksmith, a clever fellow of the name of Fraser, assumed the command. On the approach of the Earl of Loudon's army, during the night of the 16th, the smith placed his men at intervals along the roadside, and they then fired at the head of the advancing column, raising a shout, and calling on the *Camerons* and *Macdonalds* to advance, thus giving Loudon's men to understand that they were confronted by a large body of the Prince's army. Donald *Ban* Maccrimmon, Macleod of Macleod's piper, was killed by the blacksmith's shot, close by Macleod's side. Loudon's men, thinking they had to contend against a superior force, made a hasty retreat to Inverness, which was known as the *rout of Moy*. The piper was the only person killed, and the Macleods carried his body with them to Inverness.

Donald *Ban* Maccrimmon was reputed the best piper of his day in the Highlands. When leaving Dunvegan he had a presentiment that he would never return from the expedition, and on that occasion he composed that plaintive air, " *Cha till mi tuilleadh*," or Maccrimmon's Lament, which he played on the pipe as the independent companies of the Macleods were leaving Dunvegan, while their wives and sweethearts were waving a sorrowful farewell to them. To this air Maccrimmon composed a feeling Gaelic song, the sentiments in which are brought out in the English imitation by Sir Walter Scott, which is as follows :—

Macleod's wizard flag from the grey castle sallies,
The rowers are seated, unmoored are the galleys ;
Gleam war axe and broadsword, clang target and quiver,
As Maccrimmon plays " Farewell to Dunvegan for ever !"

Farewell to each cliff, on which breakers are foaming,
Farewell each dark glen in which red deer are roaming,
Farewell lonely Skye, to lake, mountain, and river,
Macleod may return, but Maccrimmon shall never.

Farewell the bright clouds that on Culen are sleeping ;
Farewell the bright eyes, in the fort that are weeping ;
To each minstrel delusion farewell ! and for ever—
Maccrimmon departs to return to you never.

The Banshee's wild voice sings the death dirge before me,
And the pall of the dead for a mantle hangs o'er me ;
But my heart shall not fly, and my nerve shall not quiver,
Though devoted I go—to return again never !

Too oft shall the note of Maccrimmon's bewailing,
Be heard when the Gael on their exile are sailing ;
Dear land ! to the shores whence unwilling we sever
Return, Return, Return, we shall never !

Maccrimmon had a sweetheart at Dunvegan, who, on hearing him play his " Lament," is said to have composed a touching song in response, which appeared in *Cuairtear nan Gleann*, and which is quoted below. It is, however, alleged that the late Rev. Dr Norman Mac-

leod of St Columba's, Glasgow, the genial and talented
editor of the *Cuairtear*, was himself the composer of the
song :—

> *Dh'iadh ceo nan stue mu aodann Chuilinn,*
> *'Us sheinn a' bhean-shith a torman mulaid,*
> *Tha suilean gorm ciuin 's an Dun a' sileadh*
> *O'n thriall thu bh' uainn 's nach till thu tuilleadh.*
> > *Cha till, cha till, cha till Maccruimein,*
> > *'An cogadh no sith cha till e tuilleadh,*
> > *Le airgiod no ni cha till Maccrumein*
> > *Cha till gu brath gu la' na cruinne.*

> *Tha osag nan gleann gu fann ag imeachd ;*
> *Gach sruthan 's gach allt gu mall le bruthach ;*
> *Tha ialt' nan speur feadh gheugan dubhach,*
> *A' caoidh gu'n d'fhalbh 's nach till thu tuilleadh.*
> > *Cha till, cha till, &c.*

> *Tha'n fhairge fa dheoidh lan broin 'us mulaid,*
> *Tha 'm bata fo sheol, ach dhiult i siubhal ;*
> *Tha gair nan tonn le fuaim neo-shubhach,*
> *Ag radh gu'n d' fhalbh 's nach till thu tuilleadh.*
> > *Cha till, cha till, &c.*

> *Cha chluinnear do cheol 's an Dun mu fheasgar,*
> *'S mac-talla nam mur le muirn 'g a fhreagairt ;*
> *Gach fleasgach 'us oigh, gu'n cheol, gu'n bheadradh,*
> *O'n thriall thu bh' uainn 's nach till thu tuilleadh.*
> > *Cha till, cha till, &c.*

On the approach of the Prince's army, the Earl
of Loudon retired with his men from Inverness to
Ross-shire, where he was pursued by a large force
under the Earl of Cromarty, among whom were the
regiment of the Mackinnons. The pursuit was afterwards entrusted to the Duke of Perth, who followed
Loudon's forces into Sutherlandshire, and broke them
up. Loudon made for the sea coast with the Macleods,
from whence they embarked for Skye. He and the
Lord President were happy to find a refuge in Skye,
and remained there, in safe quarters, until after the
battle of Culloden.

Upon the 16th day of April 1746, *Culloden Day*, the
fate of the Prince's cause was doomed after a short
but fierce struggle, in which his army had to contend
against many disadvantages, and a superior force, as

to numbers and equipments. The battle took place on Drummossie moor, near Culloden. Thereafter the "bonnie Prince Charlie" became " a hunted wanderer on the wild," with a price of thirty thousand pounds upon his head.

CHAPTER XIX.

FROM Culloden Prince Charles made his escape to Borrodale, on the shores of Lochnanuagh, where, nine months before, he had landed with high hopes. He sent to Kinlochmoydert for an old Skyeman, Donald Macleod of Gualtergill, a very respectable and trustworthy person, and who had just been engaged in piloting Æneas Macdonald, the Paris banker, to and from Barra, where he had been taking delivery of a large sum of French money, landed there for the Prince's use. Donald Macleod instantly obeyed the message, and set out for Borrodale. The first man he met with there was the Prince, walking in a wood alone. " The Prince making towards Donald asked ' Are you Donald Macleod of Gualtergill in Skye?' ' Yes,' said Donald, ' I am the same man may it please your Majesty, at your service. What is your pleasure wi' me?' ' Then,' said the Prince, ' you see Donald I am in distress. I therefore throw myself into your bosom, and let you do with me what you like. I hear you are an honest man, and fit to be trusted.' Donald made this return to the Prince, ' Alas! may it please your Excellency, what can I do for you? for I am but a poor auld man, and can do very little for mysell.' ' Why,' said the Prince, ' the service I am to put you upon I know you can perform very well. It is, that you may go with letters from me to Sir Alexander Macdonald, and the Laird of Macleod. I desire therefore to know if you will undertake this piece of service ; for I am really convinced that these gentlemen for all that they have done, will do all in their power to protect me.'"—(Jacobite Memoirs, p. 377.) Macleod refused to enter on this undertaking, as even then Sir Alexander Macdonald and Macleod of Macleod were in search of the Prince, but said he would be happy to serve the Prince in any other way. Charles then asked Macleod to pilot him to the Long Island, and accordingly, on the evening of the 26th of April, an eight-oared boat was launched and manned at Lochnanuagh, and Charles, accompanied by Captains O'Sullivan, O'Neil, and Allan Macdonald (a Catholic priest), went on board, and they set sail for the Long Island, having old Donald Macleod as pilot. One of the eight boatmen was Murdoch Macleod, a son of Donald's, and only about fifteen years of age. He had been attending the Grammar School at Inverness, but hearing that there was likely to be a battle in the neighbourhood, he ran off from school, provided himself with pistol, dirk, and claymore, and appeared on the Prince's side on the day of Culloden. After the defeat he was able to trace the Prince to Borrodale, where he met his father. After a most stormy and dangerous voyage, the Prince's party landed next morning at Rossinish, in the Island of Benbecula. From thence the Prince had adventurous voyages and wanderings to Harris and the Lewis, and back again to Benbecula, in all of which old Donald Macleod acted as his faithful guide. From Benbecula the Prince sent Donald Macleod to the mainland, with despatches to Lochiel and Secretary Murray. He returned with answers after an absence of eighteen days, and found the Prince in a hut, called the Forest House, in Glencoridale, South Uist, where he was frequently waited on by old Clanranald and his brother Boisdale, who showed him much kindness. The ladies of these gentlemen also supplied the Prince with many necessaries, and contributed to his comfort during the several weeks he passed at Glencoridale. Lady Margaret Macdonald, who was secretly attached to the Prince's interests, sent the newspapers of the day to Hugh Macdonald of Baleshare, for the purpose of being delivered to the Prince, and was forming plans for his future safety. The Government authorities having ascertained that the Prince was in the Long Island, resolved, in the hopes of securing his person, to send several companies of militia and regulars to search the outer islands, and prevent his escape therefrom. Lady Margaret becoming apprised of this, sent information to Baleshare, requesting him to communicate it personally to the Prince, and to assist in his escape. Though Baleshare was himself the captain of one of the companies of militia raised to suppress the rebellion, he entered heartily into the project of befriending the Prince, and in company with Boisdale had an interview with him at Glencoridale. Notwithstanding that the Prince's position was getting more dangerous, he made merry with his friends for three days and three nights. Baleshare had the manliness to tell the Prince at this interview, that Popery and arbitrary government were the two greatest objections against him with those who did not espouse his cause. The Prince wrote a letter of thanks and compliments to Lady Margaret, which he delivered to Baleshare on leaving. Baleshare enclosed the letter in another which he sent to his brother, Captain Donald Roy Macdonald, in which he stated that the Prince would soon leave the Long Island and land on the small isle of Fladdachuan, on the north coast of Troternish, then inhabited by one tenant and his family. Baleshare requested that both letters should be thrown into the fire after perusal. Captain Roy Macdonald was at this time residing with and under the treatment of Dr John Maclean at Shulista, in Troternish, he having, when walking off the field at Culloden, "received a musket bullet in at the sole of the left foot, and out at the buckle," and having travelled home to Skye hastily in this state, the wound took a long time to heal. On returning to Skye he made a sham surrender of his arms to Lieutenant Macleod of Balmeanach—having purchased some inferior weapons he delivered these up,

while he managed to have his own arms, which were
of superior make, secretly conveyed to his brother of
Baleshare.   On account of this surrender, Captain
Donald Roy Macdonald was allowed more freedom in
going about than others who had been out in the rebellion, and who even had not made themselves so conspicuous in the enterprise.   Sir Alexander Macdonald
was at this time at Fort-Augustus, in attendance on
the Duke of Cumberland.   It is said that when the
Duke met him, he exclaimed, " Ho ! Is this the great
rebel of the Isles."   Sir Alexander aptly replied, " No,
my Lord Duke, for had I been the rebel of the Isles
your Grace would not have crossed the Spey."   Lady
Margaret had a difficult part to perform in his absence,
for while she sympathised with the Prince in his distress, and was taking steps to further his escape, she
was surrounded by officers in the Government service,
whom she had to countenance and entertain.   Captain
Donald Roy found an opportunity of delivering the
Prince's letter into Lady Margaret's own hands, and
begged her to put it into the fire on reading it.   " No !"
she exclaimed, " I will not burn it.   I will preserve it
for the sake of him who wrote it to me.   Although
King George's forces should come to the house I hope
I shall find a way to secure the letter."   She carefully
laid it up, but was unable to keep her resolution, for
about three weeks thereafter, on the approach of Capt.
Ferguson and his red coats in search of the Prince, to
prevent discovery she threw it into the fire, which she
afterwards much regretted, as he did not search for
papers.   Acting on the information in Baleshare's
letter to his brother, that the Prince intended landing
at Fladdachuan, Lady Margaret provided twenty guineas
in gold and silver, and six of Sir Alexander's shirts,
which she delivered to Donald Roy for the Prince's
use.   Thus provided, Donald Roy set out in a boat for
Fladdachuan, ostensibly for the purpose of fishing and
gathering shells to make lime.   He landed and remained for a night on the island, but finding that no

stranger ha darrived there, he put the shells on board his boat and left the island. From thence he made his men row to the high rocky islet called *Bord Cruinn* (the round table), about a mile distant from Fladda-chuan. This is a remarkable rock, difficult to ascend, and level at the top, where there was a small hut in which, in the year 1715, one man resided, who was in charge of Sir Donald Macdonald's charters, which were there placed for safety. Donald Roy supposed the Prince might possibly land here, and though still lame, he managed to ascend the rock and satisfy himself that no one was there. He then went back to Monkstadt and returned to Lady Margaret the shirts and money, narrating to her the unsuccessful result of his voyage. From Monkstadt he returned to Dr Maclean's house at Shulista, a distance of four miles.

Meanwhile, the Prince, after Baleshare's visit, was wandering with his company between Glencoridale and Benbecula, watching and eluding the Government officials that were on his track. Macdonald of Boisdale, from whom he expected assistance and advice, was himself apprehended, and on hearing this, and that the country was over-run with soldiers, on the 24th June, Charles left Glencoridale for Benbecula, taking none with him but Captain O'Neal. On parting with Donald Macleod the Prince gave him a draft on Mr John Hay of Restalrig for sixty pistoles, which, however, he had not an opportunity of presenting, for on the 5th July Donald Macleod was taken prisoner in Benbecula by Lieutenant Allan Macdonald of Sleat. From the Long Island he was taken to Bracadale and Portree in Skye, and from thence to Applecross bay, where he was put on board the notorious Captain Ferguson's ship. Here he was brought before General Campbell, who examined him minutely as to what he knew of the Prince. Donald admitted he had been in his company, but declared that should he have got England and Scotland for his pains, he would not allow a hair of his head to be touched if he could help it. Campbell pointed to the machine called a *Barisdale,* which might be put in use if he refused to give any information he was possessed of. Donald replied that he would tell anything he knew without any machine whatsoever. There was now less danger of his doing so, as he knew the Prince was by that time beyond General Campbell's reach. The *Barisdale* was an iron machine with which Macdonald of Barisdale used to torture thieves to make them confess. "When in the machine their hands, feet, and neck, were fixed in such a manner, that the posture the man was forced to remain in was neither sitting, lying, kneeling, or standing, but, though debarred the least use of his hands and feet, his neck was somewhat more at liberty, but then he had a great weight upon the back of his neck, to which if he yielded in the least, by shrinking downwards, a sharp spike would run into his chin." Donald Macleod was carried a prisoner to London, and was confined for several months in a ship on the Thames, opposite to Tilbury Fort. He was liberated on 10th June 1747, and was presented by Mr John Walkingshaw of London with a handsome silver snuff box, of which the following description is given in the "Jacobite Memoirs," p. 410 :—" The box is an octagon oval, of three inches and three quarters in length, three inches in breadth, and an inch and a quarter in depth, and the inside of it is doubly gilt. Upon the lid is raised the eight-oared boat, with Donald at the helm, and the four under his care, together with the eight rowers distinctly represented. The sea is made to appear rough and tempestuous. Upon one of the extremities of the lid there is a landscape of the Long Isle, and the boat is just steering into Rushven, the point of Benbecula where they landed. Upon the other extremity of the lid there is a landscape of the end of the Isle of Skye, as it appears opposite to the Long Isle. Upon this representation of Skye are marked there two places, viz., Dunvegan and Gualtergill. Above the boat the clouds are represented heavy and lowering, and the rain is falling from them. The motto above the clouds, *i.e.,* round the edge of the lid by the hinge, is this, ' Olim haec meminisse juvabit, Aprilis 26to 1746.' The inscription under the sea, *i.e.*, round the edge of the lid by the opening, is this, ' Quid Neptune, paras ? Fates agitamur iniquis.' Upon the bottom of the box are carved the following words, ' Donald Macleod of Gaultergill, in the Isle of Sky, the faithful Palenurus. Æt. 68, 1746.' Below these words there is, very prettily engraved, a dove with an olive branch in her bill."

CHAPTER XX.

Kind Providence to thee a friend,
A lovely maid did timely send,
To save thee from a fearful end,
Thou charming Charlie Stuart.

THE celebrated Flora Macdonald was the daughter of Ranald Macdonald younger of Milton, in South Uist, a cadet of the Clanranald family. Her mother was Marion, daughter of the Reverend Angus Macdonald, at one time minister of Gigha, and afterwards of South Uist. This clergyman, from his great personal strength, was generally called " *A' ministear laidir.*" He was a son of Macdonald of Griminish, in North Uist (*Mac-Huisdean Ghriminish*), and was married to a daughter of Macdonald of Largie, in Cantyre. Flora Macdonald was born in 1722. Her father died when she was quite a child, and her mother was married a few years after that event to Hugh Macdonald (*Huisdean MacShomhairle*) of Armadale, Sleat. Flora had two brothers, Ranald, who was accidentally shot, when a young man, in the island of Cara, Argyllshire, and Angus, afterwards of Milton. After her mother's second marriage Flora resided with her in Skye, where she received the elements of a sound education in one of the local schools, which she completed in Edinburgh, where she resided a few years for that purpose.

At the time of the Prince's wanderings in the Long Island, Flora, who had lately returned from Edinburgh, was paying a visit to her brother Angus, at Milton, where he had just then taken up house. She was then " about 24 years of age, of a middle stature, well shaped, and a very pretty, agreeable person, of great sprightliness in her looks, and abounded with good sense, modesty, gentleness, and humanity."—(Ascanius, p. 167.) She became aware of the situation of the Prince when on a visit to Clanranald and his lady, who resided at Ormaclate House, within four miles of Milton, and they solicited her help in effecting his escape from the Long Island, which was getting too hot for him. Flora entered heartily into the dangerous undertaking, and she was enabled to carry it out with fidelity and courage. She had a meeting with the Prince and O'Neal after their leaving Glencoridale, in a hut in the island of Benbecula, and it was then arranged that she would convey the Prince, who was to attend her in disguise, to Skye. Flora then set off to Clanranald's house to make preparations for the journey. At the ford between Benbecula and South Uist, a company of militia made prisoners of her and her attendant, Niel Maceachen, as they had not a passport. Finding that the party of militia formed part of the company commanded by her stepfather, Captain Hugh Macdonald of Armadale, she refused to answer any questions until she should see their captain, who was then at some distance, and consequently she and Maceachen remained prisoners in the guard-house that night. Next day (Sunday) her stepfather arrived, and was not a little surprised to find her there under arrest. She made known to him what she was about, and he, being secretly well affected towards the Prince, at once liberated her, and gave her a passport to Skye for herself, her manservant Niel Maceachen, and a female designed " Betty Burke, an Irish girl," whom he recommended to his wife at Armadale, as a good spinster of lint and wool. This Niel Maceachen, though then in the guise of a

servant, was a man of education, having been educated
in the Scots College in Paris. He afterwards accompanied the Prince to France, and became the father of
the gallant Marshal Macdonald, Duke of Tarentum.
Lady Clanranald furnished Miss Flora with " a flowered
linen gown, a light coloured quilted petticoat, a white
apron, and a mantle of dun camlet," as a disguise for
the Prince, who now parted with his remaining companion, O'Neal, and on the evening of Saturday the
28th June, embarked with Miss Flora on board a boat
at Benbecula, and besides the boatmen, they formed
with Maceachen the only passengers. Next morning
they arrived in safety at Kilbride, near Sir Alexander
Macdonald's seat of Monkstadt. Miss Flora and Maceachen went to the house of Monkstadt, leaving the
Prince near the beach, dressed in his female attire.
Lady Margaret was somewhat prepared for Miss Flora's
account of the enterprise she was engaged in, as she
had heard by Mrs Captain John Macdonald of Kirkibost, North Uist, who had crossed the Minch the
previous day, that the Prince was about leaving the
Long Island, and she at once set about devising what
was best to be done. The difficulty at that moment
was greater as Lieutenant Macleod of Balmeanach, an
officer of one of the independent companies stationed
in the neighbourhood, was in the house, and a few of
his men were about the offices. Miss Flora entered
into conversation with this officer, and answered his
enquiries in such a manner as to disarm suspicion.
Fortunately, Alexander Macdonald of Kingsburgh, Sir
Alexander's factor, was at Monkstadt, and he being a
man of superior judgment and discretion, Lady Margaret had no hesitation in consulting him as to what
was to be done. Captain Donald Roy Macdonald, who
had been sent for by her ladyship, also arrived, and
Kingsburgh and he arranged that it would be best to
conduct the Prince to the island of Raasay, and place
him under the protection of the old laird, who was
himself in hiding among friends. Captain Roy Mac-

donald was despatched to seek out "*Rona*," as John Macleod, the young laird of Raasay, was styled, and make the necessary enquiries of him, and 'thereafter to await the Prince at Portree. Lady Margaret requested Kingsburgh to conduct the Prince to his own house that night, and Kingsburgh accordingly, after having been provided with wine and bread for the use of the Prince, sought him out, and found him seated in a secluded spot with a large knotted stick in his hand, ready to repel any attack on him. Kingsburgh explained who he was, and after the Prince had partaken of the refreshments provided, the two set out for Kingsburgh House. On the way they were overtaken by Miss Flora and Mrs John Macdonald, who were on horseback, and their attendants. They kept company for some time, but as "Betty Burke's" awkward manner was attracting attention they parted company, Kingsburgh and the Prince taking an unfrequented path to the house over the hills, arriving at Kingsburgh about midnight, Miss Flora being there a few minutes before them. All the inmates had gone to bed, and were with difficulty put up. When this had been done, however, Lady Kingsburgh (Florence, daughter of John Macdonald of Castleton) gave the Prince a cordial reception, and entertained him to an excellent supper, at which Miss Flora was placed by the Prince upon his right hand, and Lady Kingsburgh on his left. After the ladies retired, the Prince and Kingsburgh enjoyed themselves in partaking of a few rounds of whisky toddy. Meanwhile Miss Flora related her adventures to Lady Kingsburgh, who expressed her sense of the imprudence of allowing the boat's crew that brought them to Skye go back to Uist so soon, as on their arrival there they would likely be seized, and a clue found to the Prince's whereabouts. This suggestion led Miss Flora to desire the Prince next day to change his dress, which he was glad to do, having experienced its awkwardness on the previous day. Lady Kingsburgh's conjecture proved true, for the

boatmen on their return were apprehended, and a confession of all they knew about the Prince extorted from
them by threats, which led Captain Ferguson to sail
for Skye, and pursue the Prince's track from his landing at Monkstadt until he lost trace of him at Portree.
The Prince enjoyed the luxury of a comfortable bed at
Kingsburgh, and slept so soundly that Miss Flora,
anxious for his safety, prevailed on Kingsburgh to call
him up, it being then one o'clock in the afternoon.
On being asked how he had rested, he replied " Never
better ; for I thought I never lay on so good a bed, and
to tell the truth, I had almost forgot what a bed was."
In the evening the Prince took a tender farewell of his
landlady, acknowledging the kindness and hospitality
he had received under her roof ; and left the house in
the female attire he had come in there, accompanied by
Kingsburgh, who carried a suit of Highland clothes—
short coat, vest, philabeg, hose, and plaid—in a bundle
under his arm.   In a wood not far from Kingsburgh,
the Prince doffed the female habiliments and donned
the Highland dress.   He then embraced Kingsburgh,
bade him adieu, thanking him for his services, and
proceeded on his journey to, Portree, accompanied by
Niel Maceachen, and a herd boy, of the name of Macqueen, sent by Kingsburgh as a guide.   Miss Flora
went on horseback by a different road in order to gain
information and prevent discovery, and arrived at
Portree before them.   They met in the inn, kept by a
Charles Macnab, and partook of a supper of bread and
butter, cheese, and roasted fish.   Here the Prince took
leave of Miss Flora, expressing his gratitude for her
kind assistance,. and his hope that they would yet meet
at St James's.   She left next morning for her mother's
residence in Sleat, accompanied by Niel Maceachen.
About ten days thereafter she received a message from
a neighbouring gentleman, Donald Macdonald of Castleton, to come to his house ; John Macleod of Talisker,
captain of one of the independent companies, having
desired him to do so.   She went and had not proceeded

far when she met her stepfather, on his return from Uist, to whom she related all her adventures since leaving the Long Island. After parting with him, and while still on her way to Castleton, she was seized by an officer and party of soldiers, and hurried on board Captain Ferguson's cutter, the Furnace. General Campbell, who was on board, gave orders that she should be treated with every respect, and be allowed a maid servant and the use of a cabin. In about twenty days the cutter was passing Armadale, and Miss Flora was allowed to land, under escort, and take leave of her friends. She staid on shore about two hours, and after procuring the necessary outfit and engaging a girl named Kate Macdowall as maid, she returned again to the ship. She was in a day or two thereafter transferred to the Eltham, commanded by Commodore Smith, who treated her with the greatest politeness and kindness, "for which, at his request, while she was in London, she consented to sit for her picture." This ship lay for some time in Leith Roads, where Miss Flora was waited upon by several ladies, who showed her much kindness and respect. On 28th November 1746 she was put on board the Royal Sovereign, lying at the Nore, and removed to London in custody of William Dick, a messenger, in whose family she remained in honourable captivity until the passing of the act of indemnity in July 1747, when she was discharged and returned to Scotland. On her liberation she was entertained in London by Lady Primrose of Dunnipace, where she was visited by a large number of the nobility, among whom she conducted herself with the greatest propriety and ease. A testimonial amounting to several hundred pounds was raised for her in London, and Lady Primrose provided a post-chaise to convey her to Edinburgh.

After Miss Flora's return to Skye, she was married on 6th November 1750, to Mr Allan Macdonald, son of old Kingsburgh, and then residing at Flodigarry. The wedding festivities were conducted on an extensive scale, lasting three days, and the company consisted of most of the ladies and gentlemen resident in Skye, and many from the Long Island. Flora and her husband resided at Flodigarry until the death of her father-in-law, old Kingsburgh, in 1772, when she became the lady of Kingsburgh house. There, in the following year, she entertained Dr Samuel Johnson and Boswell. Johnson in his " Journey" introduces her name as one " that will be mentioned in history, and if courage and fidelity be virtues, mentioned with honour." He describes her personal appearance in these words :— " She is a woman of middle stature, soft features, gentle manners, and elegant presence." Boswell in his " Journal" writes thus of her husband :—" Kingsburgh was completely the figure of a gallant Highlander, exhibiting ' the graceful mien and manly looks' which our popular Scotch songs have justly attributed to that character. He had his tartan plaid thrown about him, a large blue bonnet with a knot of black ribband like a cockade, a brown short coat of a kind of duffil, a tartan waistcoat with gold buttons and gold button-holes, a bluish philabeg and tartan hose. He had jet black hair tied behind, and was a large stately man, with a steady sensible countenance." Not long after this visit, Kingsburgh being somewhat embarrassed in his affairs, and influenced by the then prevalent desire for emigration, left his native isle with his family, and settled in North Carolina, where he purchased a small estate. The fame of the heroine had preceded her in America, and on her arrival at Wilmington, and at various places along her route to Cross Creeks, the capital of the Highland settlement, Flora Macdonald was welcomed with martial airs and Highland honours, and every kindness shewn to her family. They had been only a few months settled in their new home, when, in 1775, the War of Independence in America broke out, and the Governor of North Carolina, calculating upon the influence of Flora among the Scotch, commissioned Donald Macdonald, who had been an officer in the

Prince's army in 1745, to raise the 84th or Royal Highland Emigrant Regiment, and gave Kingsburgh the rank of a captain in it. Flora accompanied her husband when the regiment, consisting entirely of Highlanders and sons of Highland emigrants, assembled to the number of fifteen hundred, at Cross Creeks, and she remained in the camp inspiring the men with enthusiasm in the Royal cause, until the troops began their march. A few months thereafter, this regiment was routed after a severe engagement with a superior number of the Provincial forces, under Caswell and Sillington, and the officers, including Kingsburgh, were taken prisoners and committed to the jail of Halifax. This untoward event threw Flora into deep distress, especially as none of her large family were with her to comfort her, with the exception of her daughter Frances, who was then not old enough to sympathize with her. Her five sons, Charles, Alexander, Ronald, James, and John, were all engaged in the service of their sovereign, as officers in the war then going on, and her eldest daughter, Anne, was recently married to Major Alexander Macleod, who was also engaged in the war. Flora bore these trials for a considerable time with fortitude, but at length, at the urgent request of her husband, whom she was not even permitted to see, she agreed to return with her daughter, Frances, to Scotland, he promising to rejoin her as soon as he was liberated. She sailed from Charleston, and in crossing the Atlantic, the ship in which she sailed was attacked by a French privateer, and an action ensued. While the other lady passengers confined themselves below, Flora remained on· deck animating the sailors by her voice and example, and assuring them of success. The enemy were beaten of, but in the bustle Flora was thrown down and her left arm broken. She afterwards observed that she perilled her life for the House of Stuart and for the House of Brunswick, and received little for her pains. On her return to Scotland, Flora resided on her brother's farm of Milton, South Uist, until, on the treaty of peace with

America in 1783, her husband was liberated, and joined her there. They remained in Milton only while the house of Kingsburgh was being prepared to receive them. Kingsburgh was now on the half-pay list as a captain, and he and his lady passed the remainder of their lives in the old home of Kingsburgh in comfort and happiness. Flora died on the 5th March 1790. Her remains were shrouded in one of the sheets in which Prince Charles had lain in Kingsburgh, and which she had carried with her through all her adventures from the time she left Skye for America. She was interred in the burying-ground of the Kingsburgh family, in the Church-yard of Kilmuir. So highly was she respected, and her death lamented by all classes, that several thousands attended her funeral, the procession being upwards of a mile in length, and preceded by several pipers, who played those feeling " Laments," or *Coronach*, usual on such occasions. The whole company were liberally served with refreshments in the real old Highland manner. Kingsburgh survived her for a few years, and died on the 20th September 1795. Their five sons had all distinguished themselves in the military service of their country. Charles was a captain in the Queen's Rangers. At his funeral, Lord Macdonald, on seeing his remains lowered into the grave, remarked, " There lies the most finished gentleman of my family and name." The second son, Alexander, also an officer, was lost at sea. Ronald, the third son, was a captain in the navy, " of high professional character, and remarkable for the elegance of his appearance." The fourth son, James, served with distinction as an officer in Tarlton's British Legion, and the last survivor of these martial sons was John Macdonald of Exeter, Lieutenant-Colonel of the Royal Clan Alpine Regiment, and Commandant of the Royal Edinburgh Artillery. He was the author of several works on military subjects, and was admitted a Fellow of the Royal Society. He married a daughter of Sir Robert Chambers, Chief Justice of the Supreme Court of

Judicature in Bengal. He died at Exeter on 16th August 1831, aged 72 years.

CHAPTER XXI.

CAPTAIN ROY MACDONALD, after leaving Monkstadt, rode to Tottrome and Tote, in quest of young Raasay, and having missed him at these places he proceeded to Portree, where they fortunately met, and took a walk into the fields, and then the Captain inquired of him where his father was to be found. He was much disappointed to be informed that he had gone to Knoydart. Young Raasay, however, on hearing that the Prince was still safe and in the neighbourhood, volunteered to conduct him to the island of Raasay, where he could remain concealed until he would send an express to and hear from his father, who, he was sure, " would run any risk, and be glad of an opportunity, to serve the Prince, especially in his distress." They were, however, at a loss how to have the Prince conveyed to Raasay, as they were afraid to trust a Portree crew, and as all the boats belonging to the young laird had been destroyed or carried away by the military. There were, however, two boats belonging to Captain Malcolm Macleod, young Raasay's cousin, concealed in the island, but the difficulty was how to send across for one of these. Murdoch Macleod, Raasay's third son, who had been wounded at Culloden (having received a musket bullet in at one shoulder, which made its way under the skin by the root of the neck to the other shoulder, where it lodged, until extracted by Dr Balfour, surgeon to the Macgregors in the Prince's army), was at this time residing with his sister, Mrs Macqueen, at Tottrome, and he being informed of the difficulty in getting the Prince to Raasay, said he would risk his life once more for Prince Charles, and it having occurred to him that there was a little boat on one of the fresh water lochs near Tottrome, he and his brother, with the help of some women, brought it with considerable difficulty to the sea. In this tiny craft the gallant brothers, with the assistance of a little boy, rowed across the Sound to Raasay. They fortunately found their cousin Malcolm on their landing, and he at once got ready one of his boats, which was manned by two stout boatmen, John Mackenzie and Donald Macfriar, who had previously been in the Prince's service, the one as sergeant, and the other as a private soldier. Captain Malcolm advised young Raasay not to implicate himself in the business, and that Murdoch and himself, who had already been publicly engaged in the Prince's cause, should go on this expedition. Young Raasay, however, insisted on going should it cost him the estate and his head. The five then put off to sea, and in a short time landed about half a mile from Portree. The brothers remained at the boat, while Captain Malcolm and Macfriar went to look for the Prince, who had by this time left the inn in company with Captain Roy Macdonald. They met, and Captain Roy Macdonald introduced Malcolm Macleod to the Prince as a captain in his army. They proceeded to the boat, and the names of young Raasay and his brother having been announced to the Prince " he would not permit the usual ceremonies of respect, but saluted them as his equals." The Prince here took leave of Captain Roy Macdonald, whom he wished to accompany him, as he was still anxious to have a Macdonald along with him. The captain replied that on account of his wounded foot he could not be of much service, but could further his interest more by remaining in Skye to get intelligence, and give an alarm in case the troops should discover his retreat to Raasay. The captain left Portree next morning (1st July), and called at Kingsburgh and Monkstadt to inform Kingsburgh and Lady Macdonald of the Prince's getting privately to Raasay. A few years thereafter Captain Roy Macdonald emigrated to America, where it is said he was shot at and tomahawked, while bathing, by some wild Indians. Bishop Forbes describes Captain Roy Macdonald as " a tall, sturdy man, about six foot high, and exceedingly well shaped." He was an accomplished gentleman, and had received a liberal education.

The Prince's party landed at Glam, in Raasay, opposite Portree. As most of the houses in Raasay had been burnt by the soldiers of the Government, there was considerable difficulty in finding a lodging for the Prince. A hut recently erected by some shepherds was repaired to, and young Raasay having gone in quest of provisions, soon returned with a lamb and a kid in his plaid. The kid was roasted and ate with butter, cream, and oaten bread, which repast the Prince relished much. He slept on a bed of heather prepared for him, after the primitive Highland mode, the stalks placed upright with the bloom uppermost :—

While they were in the hut, Mackenzie and Macfriar, the two boatmen, were placed as sentinels upon different eminences ; and one day an incident happened which must not be omitted. There was a man wandering about the island selling tobacco. Nobody knew him, and he was suspected to be a spy. Mackenzie came running to the hut, and told that this suspected person was approaching. Upon which the three gentlemen—young Raasay, Dr Macleod, and Malcolm—held a council of war upon him, and were unanimously of opinion that he should instantly be put to death. Prince Charles, at once assuming a grave and even severe countenance, said, " God forbid that we should take away a man's life, who may be innocent, while we can preserve our own." The gentlemen, however, persisted in their resolution, while he as strenuously continued to take the merciful side. John Mackenzie, who sat watching at the door of the hut, and overheard the debate, said in Erse, "Well, well, he must be shot ; you are the King, but we are the Parliament, and will do what we choose." Prince Charles seeing the gentlemen smile, asked what the man had said, and being told it in English, he observed that he was a clever fellow, and, notwithstanding the perilous situation in which he was, laughed loud and heartily. Luckily the unknown person did not perceive that there were people in the hut—at least did not come to it, but walked on past it, unknowing of his risk. It was afterwards found out that he was one of the Highland army, who was himself in danger.[*]

After passing two and a half days in the island of Raasay, the Prince expressed his desire to leave it, alleging that it did not afford sufficient room for

---

[*] Boswell's Tour, p. 226.

"skulking," and accordingly the whole party set sail for Skye, landing, after a rough passage, at Nicolson's Rock, Scorrybreck, late at night. They found shelter in a byre, belonging to Mr Nicolson of Scorrybreck, where they kindled a fire, and lying down around it, partook of bread and cheese. Young Raasay went to meet Captain Roy Macdonald, according to a previous appointment. The Prince slept till noon, when he rose and went out with Murdoch Macleod to "a little hill near by, where Malcolm Macleod and the two boatmen had been standing sentry. He ordered them to go in and take some sleep, of which he said they had much need, and he himself should meanwhile keep watch. He here expressed to Murdoch great anxiety for the return of his elder brother, saying he would wait for him till eight o'clock, but no longer. He then asked Murdoch if he could travel well, to which the youth replied in the negative, his wound being still unhealed. The Prince then asked if he knew his cousin, Malcolm, well, and if he was a discreet man, who might be safely trusted. Murdoch gave a strong testimony to both the discretion and fidelity of Malcolm; which seems to have determined the Prince as to his next movements." —(Chambers's Rebellion, p. 321.) He then desired Murdoch to meet him within two days at Camustian-avaig, with his own six-oared boat, an excellent sailor, to carry him off if necessary; but in the event it should be deemed unsafe for him to start from there, he wished that Captain Roy Macdonald should be desired to have another boat ready for him in Sleat. He entrusted all this to Murdoch, saying, the performance would be a piece of friendship he would never forget. He then bade Murdoch farewell, and presented him with a case containing his silver spoon, knife and fork, saying, " Keep you that till I see you."

Murdoch Macleod thereafter became a physician, and settled on the farm of Eyre, in Skye. He married Anne, daughter of Alexander Macdonald of Boisdale, by his wife Margaret, daughter of John Macdonald of

Castleton, Skye. Mrs Macleod was educated in Dublin, and was a very accomplished and agreeable lady. Dr Johnson and Boswell visited Dr Macleod's house when on their tour. Boswell writes, " We had a dish of tea at Dr Macleod's, who had a pretty good house, where was his brother, a half-pay officer. His lady was a polite, agreeable woman. Dr Johnson said he was glad to see that he was so well married, for he had an esteem for physicians. The doctor accompanied us to Kingsburgh." Dr Macleod had a family of three sons and two daughters. His eldest son, Malcolm, died in the West Indies. His second son, John, was a Lieutenant in the Navy, and the youngest, Norman, was a Lieutenant in the 92d, or Gordon Highlanders, of which regiment his uncle, Donald Macdonald of Boisdale, was major. Lieutenant Norman fought under Sir Ralph Abercromby at the battle of Aboukir, in Egypt, on 13th March 1801. " The French opened a heavy fire of cannon and musketry, which the 92d quickly returned, firmly resisting the repeated attacks of the French line (supported as it was by a powerful artillery), and singly maintaining their ground, till the line came up."—(Stewart's Sketches, p. 445.) In this action Lieutenant Norman was severely wounded, and he died in April following, of his wounds. Dr Macleod's eldest daughter, Margaret, was married to Kenneth Macleod of Swordale, afterwards of Ebost, of whom the late Murdoch Macleod, M.D., of the 11th Native Infantry, India, the late Donald Macleod, planter, in Demerara, who distinguished himself in suppressing an insurrection of the blacks there, in 1824, the Rev. Norman Macleod, F.C. Minister, North Uist, and several daughters. The doctor's youngest daughter, Anne, was unmarried, and continued, after her father's death, to reside in his house of Eyre, until in 1846 she went to live in the Free Church Manse of Snizort, with her relative, the late Reverend Roderick Macleod, where she remained until her death, in 1849.

The case with the silver spoon, knife, and fork presented by Prince Charles to Dr Macleod, are now in possession of the doctor's great grandson, Charles Shaw, Esquire, Sheriff-Substitute at Lochmaddy. The spoon, knife, and fork bear each the engraved inscription " Ex Dono, C. P. R., July 3d 1746," and were given in 1839 by Miss Anne Macleod above mentioned to Mr Shaw, along with a miniature portrait of the Prince, set in a round gold case, having on the reverse side the arms of Scotland, which portrait Dr Macleod very much prized. The silver spoon, knife, and fork presented by Sir Walter Scott in name of Lady Clerk of Pennycuick to King George IV., on his visit to Scotland in 1822, as being those given by Prince Charles to Dr Macleod, must have been spurious, for Dr Macleod, who set great value on these souvenirs, preserved them carefully in his *escritoir* up to the time of his death, and they were not removed from there until his daughter handed them to her grand-nephew.

After parting with Murdoch Macleod the Prince left the byre, desiring Captain Malcolm Macleod to accompany him, and when they had walked about a mile he addressed Malcolm, " Why, Macleod, I now throw myself entirely into your hands, and leave you to do with me what you please ; only I want to go to Strath, Mackinnon's country. I hope you will accompany me, if you think you can lead me safe enough into Strath." Malcolm agreed to conduct him there, and they accordingly proceeded to travel over the hills to Strath, the Prince being disguised as Malcolm's servant. As the Prince did not consider the Laird of Mackinnon the fittest person for his present purpose, though he said he knew him " to be as good and as honest a man as any in the world," Malcolm conducted him to the house of his brother-in-law, John Mackinnon, at Ellgol, who had been a captain in the laird of Mackinnon's regiment. Here the Prince, who still passed as Malcolm's servant, *Lewis Caw*, received much kindness. When Malcolm had disclosed to his brother-in-law who *Lewis Caw* really was, it was arranged that John Mackinnon, should go to his chief and hire a boat to convey the Prince to the mainland, and he was enjoined not to divulge that he knew anything of the Prince, but to hire the boat as if solely for the use of Captain Malcolm Macleod. John, however, could not keep the secret from his chieftain, and the old laird, delighted that he had still an opportunity of serving the Prince, at once got ready his own boat, and, with his lady, set out in it to pay him their respects. Lady Mackinnon waited in a cave upon the shore, into which the chief conducted the Prince, and Malcolm, and John Mackinnon, where they all partook of an entertainment of cold meat, wine, &c., prepared by the lady. At eight o'clock at night of the 5th July, the party repaired to the boat, which was ready for sea, and after the Prince had taken a friendly smoke with Malcolm, from the *cutty* which he had used in his wanderings, and which he now allowed Malcolm to retain, he bade him a tender farewell, and insisted on his accepting ten guineas, along with a silver stock buckle. The laird and John Mackinnon, with a party of stout rowers, then sailed with the Prince to the mainland, landed him at Knoydart, from whence he was conducted by John Mackinnon to Borodale, and after two months wandering in that neighbourhood, he embarked with a few friends on board the French privateer " Bellona," which conveyed them to France.

A few days after he had parted with the Prince, Captain Malcolm Macleod was apprehended in Raasay, conveyed to Portree, where he met Donald Macleod of Gualtergill, as a fellow prisoner, and were then carried to Applecross Bay, where they were put on board the " Furnace," and after being detained a considerable time on board this and other ships, on 1st November 1746, Malcolm was removed to London, and kept in the custody of William Dick, a messenger, till July 1747, when he was discharged. " He had cleared himself of taking up arms in behalf of the Prince, by surrendering with his men according to the Duke of Cumberland's proclamation." He returned to Scotland

R

in the same post-chaise with Miss Flora Macdonald. He
was an excellent piper, and, in 1746, composed the air
" Prince Charles' Lament." In 1773 he is described
by Boswell in his Tour as then " sixty-two years of age,
hale and well proportioned, with a manly countenance,
and tanned by the weather, yet having a ruddiness in
his cheeks, over a great part of which his rough beard
extended. His eye was quick and lively, yet his look
was not fierce, but he appeared at once firm and good
humoured. He wore a pair of brogues, tartan hose
which came up only near to his knees, and left them
bare, a purple camblet kilt, a black waistcoat, a short
green cloth coat bound with gold cord, a yellowish
bushy wig, a large blue bonnet with a gold thread
button. I never saw a figure that gave a more perfect
representation of a Highland gentleman. I wished
much to have a picture of him just as he was. I found
him frank and polite, in the true sense of the word."

CHAPTER XXII.

AFTER parting with the Prince, the Laird of Mackinnon
was taken prisoner on his way back to Skye, and was
conveyed to the Thames by sea, and there, partly on
board ship, and partly in Tilbury Fort, he was detained
a close prisoner, until he was removed to the new jail
in Southwark, whence he was liberated in July 1747.
It is related that on his release, he was reminded by
the Attorney General of the debt of gratitude he owed
his Majesty, for his clemency in liberating him. He
replied:—" Had I the King in my power as I am in
his, I would return him the compliment, by sending
him back to his own country." The laird returned to
Skye, and resided at his house of Kilmaree until his
death on 7th May 1756, in his seventy-fifth year. He
was survived by two sons and a daughter—Charles,
Lachlan, and Margaret, all born after the seventy-first
year of his age. The following notice of this gallant
and veteran chieftain is given in " A Genealogical

Account of the Family of Mackinnon," in possession of a gentleman of that clan :—" John Mackinnon of Mackinnon, or *Mackinnin Dubh*, son of John *Og*, and grandson of Lachlan *Mor*, married a daughter of Archbishop Sharpe, by whom he had a son, John, hereafter mentioned. He was attainted for being engaged in the Rebellion of 1715, having been with his clan, along with the Macdonalds of Slate, at the battle of Sheriffmuir. Though still under attainder, he was also engaged in the Rebellion of 1745, and was very instrumental in enabling Prince Charles Edward to effect his escape from the West Coast to France. After the first Rebellion, the estates were purchased by the Laird of Grant, an ancient ally of the family, and, like themselves, descended from the Alpinian stock. He conveyed them to Mr Neil Mackinnon, second son of Lachlan Mackinnon of Corry, whose nephews of that family were then under age. Mr Neil Mackinnon executed a disposition of them, in favour of John Mackinnon, younger, of Mackinnon, (then the only son of the attainted chief), and the heirs male of his body, &c., whom failing to any other son, or sons, the attainted chief might have in case of a second marriage, and the heirs male of their bodies, &c., whom failing to his nearest heirs male whatsoever; all of whom failing, to the heirs whomsoever of the said John Mackinnon, younger of Mackinnon. This deed was executed in 1728. John Mackinnon, younger of Mackinnon, above mentioned, died in 1737, without male issue, and Mishnish, as *heir of provision*, took possession of the lands. He found them much emburdened, and greatly increased those burdens himself. But the old attainted chief married again, in 1743, a daughter of Macleod of Raasay. In consequence of the part he took in the Rebellion of 1745, he was confined for several years in England; but after, returning to his family, he had two sons, Charles, afterwards of Mackinnon, born in 1753, and Lachlan, who died in Jamaica unmarried. The old chief died in 1755, and

John Macleod of Raasay, the maternal grandfather* of his infant sons, was appointed by the Court of Session their tutor-dative. He immediately commenced proceedings to procure from Mishnish restitution of the estates, which he had held merely as heir of provision; and it then appeared that a private sale of the principal estate of Strath had been made by Mishnish in 1751, to the agent of Sir James Macdonald. This sale was attempted to be set aside, but ineffectually; and only the unsold estates, namely, Mishnish and Strathaird, were got back. The Tutelar Inventory, taken by Raasay, is dated 1757, and is in the presence of Lachlan Mackinnon of Corrichatachan (*i.e.*, Corry), and his uncle, Mr Neil Mackinnon, being the nearest of kin to the minor by the father's side."

Charles Mackinnon of Mackinnon succeeded his father in the chieftainship. He sold the estates which his friends had made such efforts to preserve for the family. The estate of Strathaird in Skye was purchased from him about the year 1786, by Mr Alexander Macalister, one of the sons of Ranald Macalister of Skerinish (of the Macalisters of Loupe), by his wife, Anne, daughter of Alexander Macdonald of Kingsburgh. At the time of the sale the tenantry of Strathaird offered to place the means of purchasing the estate at the disposal of Mackinnon of Corry, but their chief opposed this, saying he was resolved if the estate went out of his own family, none other of the name should possess it. On 2d April 1782, " Charles Mackinnon of Mackinnon, Esquire," was admitted a corresponding member of the Society of Antiquaries of Scotland. He was married to a daughter of Macleod of Macleod, by whom he had a son, John, who, on his death, succeeded him in the chieftainship of the clan. John Mackinnon of Mackinnon died, unmarried, in 1808. This event raised a question as to the chieftainship of the clan Mackinnon, the honour of being heir-male,

---

* John Macleod of Raasay was the *uncle*, not *grandfather*, of the young Mackinnons, his sister, Janet, being their mother.

being disputed between the late Lachlan Mackinnon of Corry, and Letterfearn (father of the present Alexander Kenneth Mackinnon, Esquire, of Corry), and the late William Alexander Mackinnon of Portswood, Hampshire, M.P. for Lymington and Rye (father of W. A. Mackinnon, junior, Esquire, late M.P. for Lymington). The family of Corry trace their descent from Charles, or *Tearlach Skianach*, the second son of Lachlan *Dubh* Mackinnon, the chief of the clan, about the close of the sixteenth century, John *Og*, third son of the said Lachlan Dubh, being the ancestor of the family of Kyle, represented by John Mackinnon, Esquire, Kyle. Charles' son and heir was Lachlan *Ruadh* Mackinnon of Gambell, tutor of Strathardil, who had two sons, Lachlan *Og* of Gambell, and Charles *Og* of Kenuachdrach, now represented in the male line by the Reverend Donald Mackinnon of Strath, whose father, the Reverend John Mackinnon, and grandfather, the Reverend Donald Mackinnon, were, in immediate succession, the respected ministers of that parish.   Lachlan Mackinnon, son of Charles *Og*, was a good bard, and an excellent musician. Mackenzie, in his " Beauties of Gaelic Poetry," writes of him :—" Altho' we have no data to ascertain the extent of his scholastic acquirements, it is obvious from a cursory glance at his productions that he was not unlettered, while the purity and critical correctness of his Gaelic furnishes proof that he studied and understood the structure of the language."   His song of the " Unlucky Dirk" *(Bhiodag Thubaisteach)*, descriptive of his luck in the ancient game of *Iomlaid num Biodag* (changing the dirks), when, instead of his own good dagger, he received an old ungainly dirk, is very amusing.   It begins :—

> *Dh' innsinn sgeul mu'n mkalairt duibh,*
> *Na 'm fanadh sibh gu foill,*
> *Mur dh' eirich do 'n chall bhreamais domh,*
> *'Nuair chaidh mi do Dhungleois ;*
> *Air bhi thall au Scalpa dhomh,*
> *Air cuilm aig Lachunn Og ;*
> *Fhuair mi bhiodag thubaisteach*
> *Le a caisein-uchda mor.*

Lachlan *Og* Mackinnon of Gambell, eldest son of Lachlan *Ruadh*, was married to a daughter of Mackenzie of Applecross. His eldest son was Lachlan Mackinnon of Corrichatachin, or *Corry*, who married Margaret, daughter of Macrae of Inverinate, the chief of that clan, by whom he had two sons, Charles Mackinnon of Corry, and Neil Mackinnon, minister of Sleat, and a daughter, Florence, married to her cousin, Alexander Macrae of Conchra and Ardacheg. Charles Mackinnon of Corry was succeeded by his son, Lachlan Mackinnon of Corry, the entertainer of Pennant and Johnson. He was thrice married. His first wife was Jane, daughter of Nicolson of Scorrybreck, by whom he had three sons, Charles, Lachlan, and John, and two daughters, Jane and Mary. His second wife was Miss Janet Macdonald; and his last wife was Mrs Anne Macdonald or Macalister, daughter of Alexander Macdonald of Kingsburgh, and relict of Ranald Macalister of Skerinish. He had no family by the two latter marriages. The latter lady had a large family to her former husband, one of whom was governor of Penang; two were colonels in the East India Company's service, and a fourth purchased Strathaird. Her eldest daughter, Flora, was married to Charles Mackinnon younger of Corry, another was married to Norman Macdonald of Scalpay, and a third to Dr Macdonald, father of Macdonald of Innesdrynich. Charles Mackinnon, younger of Corry, resided during his lifetime at Corry with his father. He died in 1774, leaving an only son, Lachlan, and two daughters, Janet, married to the Reverend Alexander Downie of Lochalsh, and Flora, married to Neil Macleod of Gesto, father of the late Kenneth Macleod of Greshornish. Lachlan Mackinnon's second son, Lachlan, was a major in the East India Company's service, and died unmarried. The third son, John, also died unmarried in 1806. Corry's eldest daughter, Jane, was married to Macdonald of Bellfinlay, grandfather of Captain Allan Macdonald of Waternish; and his youngest, daughter, Mary, was married to the Reverend Martin Macpherson of Sleat, son of the learned Dr John Macpherson of Sleat, and brother of Sir John Macpherson, Governor-General of Bengal. Pennant, in course of his tour to the Hebrides, passed two nights at Corry. " Mr Mackinnon, junior, pressed" him " to accept the entertainment of his father's house of Coire-chattachan," where, he says, he experienced " every civility from the family." In the following year Dr Johnson and Boswell paid two visits to the house in course of their tour. Boswell remarks that " Mr Mackinnon received us with a hearty welcome, as did his wife, who was what we call in Scotland a lady-like woman. . . . We here enjoyed the comfort of a table plentifully furnished, the satisfaction of which was heightened by a numerous and cheerful company ; and we, for the first time, had a specimen of the joyous, social manners of the inhabitants of the Highlands. . . . Dr Johnson was much pleased with his entertainment here. . . . Mrs Mackinnon, with unaffected hospitality and politeness, expressed her happiness in having such company in her house, and appeared to understand and relish Dr Johnson's conversation, as indeed all the company seemed to do. When I knew she was old Kingsburgh's daughter, I did not wonder at the good appearance which she made." Lachlan Mackinnon (old Corry) died in 1789, and was succeeded by his grandson, Lachlan Mackinnon (son of Charles) before mentioned. Lachlan Mackinnon of Corry and Letterfearn was for many years Sheriff-Substitute of Skye. He was present, along with his son, Farquhar Mackinnon younger of Corry, at the meeting in Inverness on 27th February 1817, establishing the Inverness Sheep and Wool Market. He stated at the meeting that " he had authority from John Macpherson, Chamberlain, Skye ; Norman Macleod of Drynoch, Niel Macleod of Gesto, the Rev. James Suter, factor for the laird of Macleod ; Ewen Macmillan, Glenbrittle ; Mr John Maclean, Braeoinart; Mr Norman Morrison, Satarn ; Mr John Gillespie,

Kilmaree ; and Mr Donald Macdonald of Skeabost, to express their approval of the proposed market." He was married to Anne, daughter of Farquhar Macrae of Inverinate, by whom he had several sons and daughters, all occupying good positions in society. The Corry family is now represented in Skye by Alexander Kenneth Mackinnon, Esquire of Corry (son of the above-mentioned Lachlan), a Deputy Lieutenant of the county of Inverness, and Chamberlain for Lord Macdonald, &c.

William Alexander Mackinnon, Esquire, the other claimant to the chieftainship of the clan Mackinnon, traces his descent from Donald, a son of Lachlan Mòr Mackinnon of Strathordell, chief of the clan towards the close of the seventeenth century. This Donald emigrated to Antigua and married Mrs Thomas, widow of the governor of the island. He died in 1720. His son, William, married a daughter of Lieutenant Governor Yeamans, of the same island, by whom he had two sons—William, his heir, and Henry, a Major-General, born in 1773, who " after achieving the highest reputation as a gallant soldier and skilful commander, particularly by his brilliant services under Wellington in the Peninsula, was killed at the storming of Ciudad Rodrigo" on 29th February 1812. There is a tablet erected to his memory in St Paul's Cathedral. William Mackinnon died young, leaving two sons, William Alexander and Daniel. William Alexander Mackinnon was born in 1789. He was for nearly forty years a member of the House of Commons. He also distinguished himself in literature, having published a work on " Public Opinion," also " Thoughts on the Currency Question," and " History of Civilisation." In 1812 he married Emma Mary, only daughter of Mr Palmer of Palmerstown, county Mayo, whose estates he inherited in right of his wife. He died in 1869, and is succeeded by his son, William Alexander Mackinnon, junior, Esquire, late M.P. for Lymington, who was born in 1813. Daniel Mackinnon attained the rank of colonel of the Coldstream Guards, of which corps he wrote a history. He was a brave and gallant soldier, and distinguished himself in the Peninsular war. In June 1815 so anxious was he, while on a visit to England, to join his regiment at Brussels, that he crossed in an open boat from Ramsgate to Ostend. On the field of Waterloo, on the 18th of that same month, he had three horses shot under him, and being entrusted by the Duke of Wellington to defend the important post of Hougomont, on that field, to the last extremity, he performed the dangerous service in the most gallant manner. He died in 1836.

It is on the other hand alleged that Donald Mackinnon, who went to Antigua, was an illegitimate son of the chief, Lachlan Mòr Mackinnon. " Donald, natural son of the said Lauchlan M'Fingoun" (Mackinnon) is mentioned in a tack of " the two and a half-penny lands of Robestoun, in the parish of Kilchrist," granted by the said Lachlan in 1688, and there was a tradition in Strath that this Donald went to the West Indies. The following correspondence on the subject of the chieftainship of the clan Mackinnon appeared in 1849 in the *Inverness Courier*. Mr James Logan, author of " The Scottish Gael," writes :—

I am aware that there is a difference of opinion respecting the chiefship of Clan 'innon, as Mr Alaster D. Mackinnon and your correspondent in Sky observe. I had the pleasure of corresponding at considerable length on this subject with the late Mr Mackinnon of Corrie, who was exceedingly well informed on the history and genealogy of his clan, but as my opinion did not agree with his, nor assimilate with that of your correspondents, will you allow me to state the reasons of dissent?

The question hinges on the fate of Donald, second son of Lachlan Mòr, who lived in the reign of Charles I., for whom he fought with his followers at the battle of Worcester, 1651. If Donald had fallen in that unfortunate field, then the representation of the old line of chiefs would have passed to the descendants of *Tearlach Sgianach*, son of Lachlan Dù, who flourished 1570-80, the head of which house is now Mackinnon of Coire Chattachan (Corrie) ; but being taken prisoner, Donald was either compelled to expatriate himself, or voluntarily emigrated to Antigua, where he married Mrs Thomas, widow of the governor of the island. His son, William, married Miss Yeamans, daughter of the Lieutenant-Governor. His son married Louisa, daughter of Henry Vernon, Esq. of Hilton Park, Staffordshire, whose son, William, married Harriet, daughter of John Tyre, Esq. of Antigua, and their elder son, William Alexander, is the gentleman whose right to the chiefship is objected to.

To this letter Mr Alaster D. Mackinnon, Corry, replied :—

In your number of the 14th inst. appeared a letter from Mr Logan on the subject of the chiefship of the Clan Mackinnon, in which he gives reasons for claiming the title of chief for W. A. Mackinnon, Esq., M P. The controversy is materially narrowed by Mr L.'s admission that if Donald, second son of Lachlan Mòr, who fought with his followers at the battle of Worcester in 1651, had fallen on that field, " then the representation of the old line of chiefs would have passed to the descendants of *Tearlach Sgianach*, son of Lachlan Dù, who flourished in 1570 80, the head of which house is now Mackinnon Coire Chattachan (Corrie)." It follows, *a fortiori*, that the right of a member of the Corrie family to be acknowledged chief is incontestible, if it can be shown that no such second son of Lachlan Mòr ever existed, or could have fought with his father at Worcester in 1651.

Lachlan Mòr was the son of John the Dumby, who married in 1627 a daughter of Maclean of Coll, which is proved by the record of a deed executed in that year. In this deed the Dumby's father grants a provision of some of his lands to Katherine, eldest daughter of Lachlean Maclean of Coll, and spouse or intended spouse to his eldest son John. Mr Neill, rector of Sleat, acted as Sir Lachlan's bailie in giving sasine to the lady. Lachlan Mòr could not have been born at all events till the year following the marriage, i.e., 1628, and therefore could not himself have been more than twenty-three years of age when the battle of Worcester was fought. That he was not older than this is further proved from the records of 1642, in which year, by a writ under the great seal dated the 16th February, John Maclean of Coll was appointed tutor-dative to his nephew, Lachlan Macfingon of Strathardell, eldest son and heir apparent of the deceased John Macfingon of Strathardell, being a pupil. So late indeed as 1648 we still find this Lachlan Mackinnon spoken of in the records as a minor. It is evident therefore he could not be the father of a man who fought in 1651 ; and that the person on whom Mr W. A. Mackinnon rests his claims of descent cannot have been a son of the chief of the day.

CHAPTER XXIII.

ABOUT a fortnight after Prince Charles was entertained at Kingsburgh house, Captain Ferguson, who was on his track, arrived there, and made Alexander Macdonald (old Kingsburgh) a prisoner. He was allowed by General Campbell to go on parole, without any guard, to Fort-Augustus, but on his arrival there he was thrown into a dungeon, and loaded with chains. From thence he was removed, under a guard of Kingston's horse, to Edinburgh Castle, and placed there in solitary confinement. Several efforts were made on his behalf. Sir Alexander Macdonald and Lady Margaret both wrote the Lord President to contribute his good offices in his behalf. Lady Margaret describes Kingsburgh as " a man well known for his singular honesty, integrity, and prudence in all occurrencies of life." Sir Alexander's letter is dated " Fort-Augustus, 29th July 1746." After narrating "the misfortune of Kingsborrow, now sent a prisoner to Edinburgh," Sir Alexander concludes :—

On arriving here, the Duke ordered Sir Everard Fawkener to examine him, and since he has been confined, and now sent to Edinburgh. I used my little Rhetoric with the Duke, but he stopt my mouth by saying, that this man had neglected the greatest piece of service that could have been done, and if he was to be pardoned, you have too much sense to think this the proper time ; as it would encourage others to follow his example. I need not tell your Lordship how much I am concerned for the man's misfortune ; nor need I beg your assistance in a thing I have so much at heart as the safety of this man, because I have always found you friendly in every thing that concerned me.

Kingsburgh was still in confinement when his kind chief died. The circumstances attending Sir Alexander Macdonald's death are narrated in the following letter from Donald Macdonald of Castleton to the Lord President, dated at Armidale, December 5th, 1746, published in the *Culloden Papers :*—

My Lord,—I believe ere this letter shall come to your hands, you shall hear of the death of Sir Alexander Macdonald, who died at Bernera, in Glenelg, on Sunday, the 23d of last month. He arrived at that place on Wednesday the 19th, was that night taken ill of pleuresy, which carried him off in four days. Your lordship's intimacy with this gentleman for many years made you thoroughly acquaint with his character ; and therefore, I shall not venture to speak much of it in this letter—only allow me to say that he was a downright honest man, true to his friend, and firm to his word. By his death we of his clan lost a father, and the King a good subject. Lady Margaret bears her affliction with that patience and resignation which becomes a Christian and a woman of prudence ; and there is nothing wherein his friends can show a greater regard for his memory, than by doing all the good offices in their power to his lady and infant children. There is, my Lord, one particular in which she has ordered me to solicite your interest, at a time she is not in a condition to write to you ; and that is in behalf of Mr Macdonald of Kingsborrow, now a prisoner in the Castle of Edinborough. That gentleman has been a principal manager of the affairs of the family of Macdonald for twenty-eight years, and did always discharge his trust with faithfullness and diligence. And, as by his long management, he is best acquainted with the affairs of the family, so there cannot be no greater service at present done her and her children, than that he should be sett at liberty, and reinstated in his former office. Your Lordship also knows how serviceable Sir Alexander Macdonald also was in suppressing the late Rebellion ; and tho' he has not lived to receive any favors suitable to his services, yet, it is hoped, they are not so forgott but that they shall be remembered to his lady and children, and they would take the liberation of the gentleman in the Castle as an earnest of the regard of the Government for them ; but how, or in what manner, this favour can be procured Lady Margaret leaves entirely to your Lordship's judgement.   I am, &c.

Sir Alexander Macdonald died in the prime of his life, and his death was much lamented.   The following elegy on him was composed by his friend, John Macleod of Drynoch :—

> He said, who dwells in uncreated light,
> Let art and nature try their skill and might.
> To form a model for the human kind,
> A body faultless, and a faultless mind :
> Obedient nature summoned all her force,
> And art, indulgent, opened every source ;
> The rival sisters all their gifts prepare,
> And grant their hero more than mortal share.
> My dear Macdonald was that very man,
> Let malice point one blemish if she can.
> Great, good, and regular his every part,
> His form majestic—godlike was his heart.
> No sordid passions harboured in his breast,
> A place too sacred for so mean a guest.
> His honour spotless,—sacred was his word ;
> His friend was master of his purse and sword.
> His acts of goodness, envy's tongue must tell
> Were such as few can equal, none excell.
> In all things just—with knowledge most refined ;
> Polite his manners, easy, unconfined.
> He 's gone in bloom of youth—Oh sad decree !
> Lost to the world,—Alas ! and lost to me.

Sir Alexander Macdonald was succeeded in the estates and title by his son, Sir James, who was only five years of age at his father's death.   He had two other sons— Alexander (afterwards Lord Macdonald), and Archibald, a posthumous child.   Lady Margaret Macdonald removed to England a few years after her husband's death, for the education of her sons.   Her youngest son, Sir Archibald Macdonald, after having been educated at Westminster School, and Christ Church,

Oxford, studied for the English Bar, and "by his talents and virtue" rose to be Lord Chief Baron of the Exchequer. He was created a Baronet of the United Kingdom on 27th November 1813. Sir Archibald was married to Louisa, eldest daughter of the Marquess of Stafford. He died in 1826, and was succeeded by his son, Sir James Macdonald, M.P. for Hampshire. He died in 1832, and is succeeded by his eldest son (by his second wife, Sophia, eldest daughter of the Earl of Albemarle), Sir Archibald-Keppel Macdonald of East Sheen, Surrey, formerly an officer in the Scots Fusilier Guards, and equerry to the late Duke of Sussex.

Sir James Macdonald is described by Sir Robert Douglas in his " Peerage of Scotland" as " a youth of extraordinary natural parts, which were greatly improved by a liberal education and travelling, of a most sweet disposition, and, for learning and knowledge in the liberal arts and sciences, inferior to none of his contemporaries." He was styled the " Scottish Marcellus," on account of his distinguished accomplishments. On his return from England to his estates, his kind, agreeable, and entertaining manner, made him deservedly popular among his clan. Old Kingsburgh was detained a prisoner in Edinburgh Castle until, by the Act of Grace, he was set at liberty on the 4th of July 1747, having thus "got a whole year's safe lodging for affording that of one night." On his liberation he became one of Sir James Macdonald's tutors and curators, in which capacity he acted until Sir James came of age. Sir James, in consideration of his long and faithful services to the family, granted him an annuity of fifty pounds sterling, which he enjoyed until his death, at the advanced age of eighty-three, on the 13th of February 1772. Kingsburgh's second son, James Macdonald of Knockow, succeeded him as factor for the Macdonald estates in Skye.

Sir James Macdonald went on a shooting excursion in 1764, to his property of North Uist, accompanied by Colonel John Macleod of Talisker, and other gentlemen from Skye. While deer-stalking at a place called *Airidh-na-gaoithe,* Colonel Macleod's gun accidentally went off, from a twig of heather having caught the trigger, and the shot lodged in Sir James's leg, on which he fell. The gentlemen present immediately procured blankets from the nearest cottages, in which he was carried over the moor, a distance of five miles, to Vallay-House, the residence of his relative, Ewen Macdonald of Vallay. Mr Macdonald, who was both a poet and a musician, composed on this occasion the air known as *Cumha na coise, i.e.,* the Lament for the Foot; with appropriate words :—

> *Mo ghaol, mo ghaol do chas threubhach,*
> *Dha 'n d'thig an t-osan 's am feileadh:*
> *Bu leat toiseach na 'n ceudan*
> *'N am feigh bhi ga'n ruith.*

The people of the island, on hearing that Sir James was wounded, suspected that Talisker had acted designedly, and they at once flew to arms and surrounded Vallay House, and would have taken Talisker's life, had not Vallay and the other Macdonald gentlemen present assured them that what had happened was purely accidental, when they were with difficulty persuaded to disband. It is said that this accident led to the devising of the guard over the trigger of guns, which is called in the Hebrides " *An t-iarunn fraoich,*" *i.e.,* the heather iron. Sir James was confined to Vallay House for several weeks by this accident, and on his recovery, Vallay, to evince his joy, composed the *piobaireachd* " Sir James Macdonald of the Isles' Salute," which he played with great taste on the bagpipe.

James Macpherson, the translator of the poems of Ossian, while on his tour in 1760 collecting these poems, visited Skye, where he procured several pieces of that most ancient heroic poetry. He was directed by the Rev. Dr Donald Macqueen of Kilmuir to Alexander Macpherson, residing near Portree, noted for his knowledge of these poems. He was engaged for four days taking down from this man's recitation poems regarding the *Fians,* or Fingalians, the composition of which were ascribed to Ossian. Alexander Macpherson also delivered to him an old Gaelic MS. volume of some of the poems of Ossian. Mrs Nicolson of Scorrybreck repeated at this time to James Macpherson a short poem, called *" Dearg MacDeirg,"* which was in the Ossianic style, but which did not appear in his translation. She recited this poem in 1802 to Lord Webb Seymour and Professor Playfair, when on their tour through the Highlands and Isles. Macpherson was assisted in his translation of Ossian by Captain Alexander Morrison, a Skyeman, and a superior Gaelic scholar. It was he who remarked that Macpherson " could as soon write the prophecies of Isaiah, or create the Isle of Skye, as compose a poem like one of Ossian's." In a letter to Dr Blair, dated the 10th October, 1763, Sir James Macdonald writes :—

Your letter to me on the subject of Ossian's poems came at a very unlucky time for giving you any assistance in the enquiry you wish to set on foot. I received your letter yesterday, and have appointed a meeting with all the people of my estate in one end of Skye to-morrow, in order to fix them in their different possessions for some time to come. . . . The few bards that are left among us repeat only detached pieces of these poems. I have often heard and understood them ; particularly from one man, called John Maccodrum, who lives on my estate of North Uist. I have heard him repeat for hours together poems which seemed to me to be the same with Macpherson's translation.

General Macleod of Macleod wrote in 1785 on this subject :—

My opinion of this controversy is that the poems certainly did exist in detached pieces and fragments ; that few of them had been committed to paper before the time of the translator ; that he collected most of them from persons who could recite them, or parts of them ; that he arranged and connected the parts, and perhaps made imitative additions for the sake of connection ; that those additions cannot be large or numerous ; and that the foundation and genuine remains of the poems are sufficiently authentic for every purpose of taste or criticism. It might be wished, for the sake of squeamish critics, that the translator had given them to the world as he found them, though as a reader I own myself delighted with Fingal and Temora in their present appearance.

In the testimony of Hugh Macdonald of Kilpheder (who was a cousin of Allan Macdonald of Kingsburgh) as to the authenticity of Ossian's poems, there is the following notice of Skye bards :—

John Maccodrum's predecessor in the office of bard to the family of Macdonald was Duncan Macruari, who possessed as bard the lands in Troternish *Acha nam bard*, or Bard's field. His descendants, as well as the collateral branches of his family, are to this day called *Clann a Bhaird*. When the chief of Macleod dismissed MacGille Riabhich, his family bard, Macdonald received him hospitably, and gave him lands in the parish of Kilmuir, in Troternish, called Baile MhicGille Riabhich.

This Hugh Macdonald was the father of the Rev. James Macdonald, author of the " Agricultural Survey of the Hebrides," who was married to a daughter of Professor Playfair.

Sir James Macdonald having become ill with consumption, was obliged to go to Italy in 1765 for the purpose of recruiting his health. He, however, succumbed to the malady after a painful and protracted illness, and died at Rome on the 26th July 1766. His character stood so high that Pope Clement XIII. ordered a public funeral, and that he should be interred in consecrated ground, an unwonted concession to a Protestant. Cardinal Picolonimi wrote an elegant Latin elegy on him ; and George Lord Lyttleton wrote the following inscription, placed on a monument executed in Rome, and erected to his memory in the parish church of Sleat :—

To the memory of Sir James Macdonald, Bart., who in the flower of youth had attained to so eminent a degree of knowledge in mathematics, philosophy, languages, and in every other branch of useful and polite learning, as few have acquired in a long life wholly devoted to study. Yet to this erudition he joined what can rarely be found with it, great talents for business, great propriety of behaviour, great politeness of manners. His eloquence was sweet, correct, and flowing ; his memory vast and exact ; his judgment strong and acute ; all which endowments, united with the most amiable temper and every private virtue, procured him not only in his own country, but also from foreign nations, the highest marks of esteem. In the year of our Lord 1766, the 25th of his life, after a long and extremely painful illness, which he supported with admirable patience and fortitude, he died at Rome, where, notwithstanding the difference of religion, such extraordinary honours were paid to his memory, as had never graced that of any other British subject since the death of Sir Philip Sydney. The fame he left behind him is the best consolation to his afflicted family, and to his countrymen in this isle, for whose benefit he had planned many useful improvements, which his fruitful genius suggested and his active spirit promoted, under the sober direction of a clear and enlightened understanding. Reader, bewail our loss, and that of all Britain ! In testimony of her love, and as the best return she can make to her departed son, for the constant tenderness and affection, which even to his last moments he showed for her, his much afflicted mother, the Lady Margaret Macdonald, daughter to the Earl of Eglintoune, erected this monument A.D. 1768.

Gaelic elegies on Sir James were also composed by his natural brother Archibald Macdonald *(Ciaran Mabach)*, who was a bard, and by the family bard, John Maccodrum of North Uist. Colonel Stewart, in his Sketches, has the following remarks on Sir James Macdonald's death :—

To a distant and unimproved region like Skye, the loss of such a man was irreparable. The example of his learning and virtues, his kindly feelings towards his people, and the encouragement and improvements he contemplated for them, would, no doubt, have produced incalculable advantages. His learning and accomplishments could have been understood and appreciated by the gentlemen farmers, tacksmen, and others of his people, who, as I have already noticed, were so well educated, that conversations were frequently carried on in the Latin language. The clergymen were also of a superior class. Born of good families, zealous in the discharge of their religious duties, and learned and exemplary in their conduct, their influence over the minds and actions of their flocks was great and beneficial. Even Dr Johnson, with all his prejudicies against Scotland and the Presbyterian clergy, could not conceal his surprise at the well-selected libraries and the learning he met with in Skye.

Sir James Macdonald was succeeded by his brother, Sir Alexander, who was elevated to the peerage of Ireland in 1776, by the title of Baron Macdonald of Sleat. Lord Macdonald, distinguished from the other Barons of his family by the appellation *"Am Morair Ban,"* or the *fair-haired lord,* being an " English bred chieftain," and severe in exacting and increasing his rents, was somewhat unpopular with his principal tenants, several of whom combined to keep the lands at the old rents, and many, feeling the pressure of the times, were forced to emigrate. Boswell, in 1773, writes, " We reached the harbour of Portree, in Skye, which is a large and good one. There was lying in it a vessel to carry off the emigrants called the *Nestor.* It made a short settlement of the differences between a chief and his clan :—

Nestor componere lites
Inter Peleiden festinat et inter Atriden."

(While hoary Nestor, by experience wise,
To reconcile the angry monarchs tries.)

Lord Macdonald was an Eton scholar, and was both talented and accomplished. He moved a good deal in literary circles, and was a member of the Society of Antiquaries. He had a great taste for music, and frequently entertained the celebrated harper, O'Kane, who used to delight him with his performances. Gunn, in his work on the harp, writes :—" No one was better able to feel and to estimate the superior talents of O'Kane, for I can vouch Lord Macdonald to have been one of our best amateurs on the violin, and one of the best judges of musical talents of that period. There had been for a great length of time in the family a valuable harp key ; it was finely ornamented with gold and silver, and with a precious stone. This key was said to have been worth eighty or one hundred guineas, and on this occasion our itinerant harper had the good fortune of being presented by Lord Macdonald with this curious and valuable implement of his profession."

In December 1777, letters of service were granted to Lord Macdonald to raise a regiment in the Highlands and Isles, of which corps he was offered the command. He declined the commission, but recommended Major John Macdonell of Lochgarry, who was accordingly appointed Lieutenant-Colonel Commandant of the regiment, which was called the Macdonald's Highlanders, or seventy-sixth regiment. Most of the men, numbering 750, were raised by his lordship's exertions and influence, and he made a good selection of officers from his own clan, and that of the Mackinnons, and other neighbouring clans. In March 1778, the regiment, then numbering 1086, was inspected at Inverness by General Skene, and reported complete. In March 1779, the regiment was at Burntisland, preparatory to embarking for America, when it was observed that great numbers of the Highlanders were, in parties, in earnest conversation. In the evening of the third day, each company gave in a written state-

ment, complaining of their bounty money being with-
held, and other non-performance of promise, and
accompanied by a declaration that, till their grievances
were redressed, they would not embark. They desired
that Lord Macdonald, the chief and patron of the
regiment, should be sent for, to see justice done to
them. Not having received a satisfactory answer so
soon as they expected, they marched in a body, and
took possession of a hill above Burntisland, firm to
their purpose, but abstaining from violence, and when
other young soldiers wished to join them, they ordered
them back to their quarters, telling them they had no
cause of complaint, and ought therefore to do their
duty and obey their officers. They remained on the
hill for some days, sending parties to the town for
provisions, which they punctually paid. An investi-
gation, by the major and paymaster, took place, when
it was found that the claims were well founded.
" When this statement was laid before Lord Macdonald
on his arrival, he advanced the money claimed by the
soldiers, which amounted to a considerable sum, taking
upon himself the risk of recovering it from those whose
conduct had nearly ruined a brave and honourable body
of men, as they afterwards proved themselves to be."—
(Stewart's Sketches.) Before the departure of the
Skyemen in the regiment, they generously sent the
money they had received home to their families and
friends. After distinguished service in the American
War, the regiment returned to Scotland, and was dis-
banded at Stirling in March 1784.

Lord Macdonald was married to Elizabeth Diana,
eldest daughter of Godfrey Bosville, Esquire of Gunthwaite, Yorkshire, by whom he had issue, seven sons
and three daughters :—Alexander Wentworth, his
successor; Godfrey, heir to his brother; James, a lieutenant-colonel in the army, killed at Bergen-op-zoom,
9th March 1814 ; Archibald, Dudley Stewart Erskine,
John Sinclair, and William ; Diana, married to Sir
John Sinclair, Bart., of Ulbster; Elizabeth, and Anna-

bella. Lady Elizabeth Diana Macdonald died on 18th October 1789, on which occasion Angus Macarthur, the family piper, composed the tune, or *piobaireachd*, " Lady Macdonald's Lament." Lord Alexander Macdonald died on 12th September 1795. His mother, the popular Lady Margaret Macdonald, survived till March 1799.

Lord Alexander Wentworth Macdonald, generally styled by his tenants *Alasdair Mor*, requested permission from King George III. to raise a regiment on his estates in the Isles. This request was readily granted and a fine body of men were soon recruited, the regiment being named " The Regiment of the Isles." It was inspected and embodied at Inverness on the 4th June 1799. " It would appear, from the selection made, that there was no want of men on Lord Macdonald's estate, as their age averaged twenty-two years, a period of life the best calculated to enter upon military service ; not too young to suffer from, or to be incapable of supporting, the hardships and fatigues peculiar to the profession, nor too old to mould the mental and personal habits of the soldier, to the moral and military restraints which the profession renders necessary."—(Stewart's Sketches.) This regiment was employed in 1801 to put down a combination amongst the seamen at Whitehaven to raise their wages by preventing vessels from leaving the harbour. No force was, however, found necessary, as from the respect in which the regiment was held, and the imposing appearance of the men when drawn up and prepared to act, the sailors were persuaded to yield their point and to return to their ships. The regiment was reduced in 1802. Lord Alexander Wentworth died, unmarried, on 19th June 1824, and was succeeded by his brother, Lord Godfrey Macdonald, who was a major-general in the army. He had four sons, viz. :—Godfrey William Wentworth, 4th Baron ; the Hon. James William Macdonald, C.B., Knight of the Legion of Honour, a Colonel in the army, Private Secretary, and A.D.C. to his Royal Highness the Duke

of Cambridge; William, who was also an officer in the
army; and Alexander W. R. Bosville, of Thorpe, and
Gunthwaite, Yorkshire. Lord Godfrey died on 12th
October 1832, and was succeeded in the title and Scotch
estates by his son, Lord Godfrey William Wentworth,
who died in 1863, aged fifty-four years, and was
succeeded by his son, the Right Honourable Somerled
James Brudenell Bosville, Lord Macdonald, of Armadale Castle, Skye, and Settrington House, Yorkshire,
the present peer.

CHAPTER XXIV.

CAPTAIN JOHN MACLEOD, younger of Macleod, and only
son of Norman Macleod of Macleod, mentioned as
actively engaged in the suppression of the rebellion of
1745, was married about 1753 to Emilia, daughter of
Alexander Brodie of Brodie, Lyon King at Arms. He
went to reside at Beverley, in Yorkshire, in 1765,
where in the following year he died and was buried in
the minster. His widow and family of daughters
removed to Hampshire, while his son, Norman Macleod, studied for five years in Edinburgh, under Professor George Stuart. From thence he removed to the
University of St Andrews, his grandfather having taken
a house in the neighbourhood of that town. Part of
his subsequent career is best given in his own words :—

In the year 1771 a strange passion for emigrating to America seized
many of the middling and poorer sort of Highlanders. The change of
manners in their chieftains since 1745, produced effects which were
evidently the proximate cause of this unnatural dereliction of their own,
and appetite for a foreign country. The laws which deprived the Highlanders of their arms and garb would certainly have destroyed the feudal
military powers of the chieftains, but the fond attachment of the people
to their patriarchs would have yielded to no laws. They were themselves
the destroyers of that pleasing influence. Sucked into the vortex of the
nation and allured to the capitals, they degenerated from patriarchs and
chieftains to landlords ; and they became as anxious for increase of rent
as the new-made lairds—the *novi homines*—the mercantile purchasers of
the Lowlands. Many tenants, whose fathers for generations had enjoyed
their little spots, were removed for higher bidders. Those who agreed,

at any price, for their ancient *lares*, were forced to pay an increased rent, without being taught any new method to increase their produce. In the Hebrides, especially, this change was not gradual but sudden, and sudden and baleful were its effects. The people, freed by the laws from the power of the chieftains, and loosened by the chieftains themselves from the bonds of affection, turned their eyes and their hearts to new scenes. America seemed to open its arms to receive every discontented Briton. To those possessed of very small sums of money it offered large possessions of uncultivated but excellent land, in a preferable climate ; to the poor it held out high wages for labour ; to all it promised property and independence. Many artful emissaries, who had an interest in the transportation or settlement of emigrants, industriously displayed these temptations ; and the desire of leaving their country for the new land of promise became furious and epidemic. Like all other popular furies, it infected not only those who had reason to complain of their situations or injuries, but those who were most favoured and most comfortably settled. In the beginning of 1772 my grandfather, who had always been a most beneficent and beloved chieftain, but whose necessities had lately induced him to raise his rents, became much alarmed by this new spirit which had reached his clan. Aged and infirm, he was unable to apply the remedy in person, he devolved the task on me, and me for an assistant our nearest male relation, Colonel Macleod of Talisker. The duty imposed on us was difficult ; the estate was loaded with debt, encumbered with a numerous issue from himself and my father, and charged with some jointures. His tenants had lost in that severe winter above a third of their cattle, which constituted their substance ; their spirits were soured by their losses, and the late augmentations of rent ; and their ideas of America were inflamed by the strongest representations, and the example of their neighbouring clans. My friend and I were empowered to grant such deductions in the rents as might seem necessary and reasonable ; but we found it terrible to decide between the justice to creditors, the necessities of an ancient family which we ourselves represented, and the claims and distresses of an impoverished tenantry. To God I owe, and I trust will ever pay, the most fervent thanks that this terrible task enabled us to lay the foundation of circumstances (though then unlooked for) that I hope will prove the means not only of the rescue but of the aggrandisement of our family. I was young and had the warmth of the liberal passions natural to that age ; I called the people of the different districts of our estate together ; I laid before them the situation of our family, its debts, its burthens, its distress ; I acknowledged the hardships under which they laboured ; I described and reminded them of the manner in which they and their ancestors had lived with mine. I combated their passion for America by a real account of the dangers and hardships they might encounter there ; I besought them to love their young chieftain, and to renew with him the ancient manners. I promised to live among them ; I threw myself upon them ; I recalled to their remembrance an ancestor who had also found his estate in ruin, and whose memory was held in the highest veneration. I desired every district to point out some of their oldest and most respected men to settle with me every claim ; and I promised to do everything for their relief which in reason I could. My worthy relation ably seconded me, and our labour was not in vain. We gave considerable abatements in the rents ; few emigrated, and the clan conceived the most lively attachment to me, which they most effectually manifested, as will be seen in course of these memoirs. When we were engaged in these affairs my grandfather died and was buried at St Andrews. I returned to Hampshire, and easily prevailed with my excellent mother and sisters to repair in performance of my promise, to my clan to Dunvegan. In my first visit to Skye Mr Pennant arrived there, and he has kindly noticed in his Tour the exertions we then made.

Pennant refers to Macleod in the following terms :— " He feels for the distresses of his people, and, insensible of his own, with uncommon disinterestedness, has relieved his tenants from the oppressive rents—has received, instead of the trash of gold, the treasure of warm affections and unfeigned prayer."

In 1773 Dr Johnson and Boswell were entertained by Macleod of Macleod, at Dunvegan Castle, in the most sumptuous manner. Johnson thus describes their reception :—" Whatever is imagined in the wildest tales, if giants, dragons, and enchantment be excepted, would be felt by him, who, wandering in the mountains without a guide, or upon the sea without a pilot, should be carried amidst his terror and uncertainty to the hospitality and elegance of Raasay or Dunvegan." Boswell wrote :—" Our entertainment here was in so elegant a style, and reminded my fellow traveller so much of England, that he became quite joyous. He laughed and said, ' Boswell, we came in at the wrong end of this island.'—' Sir,' said I, ' it was best to keep this for the last.' He answered, ' I would have it both first and last.' "

In 1776 Macleod of Macleod entered the army, and, raising an independent company, served in America. In 1780 he assisted materially in raising the second battalion of the 42d regiment, afterwards the seventy-third, of which he was appointed Lieutenant-Colonel. In 1781 he led this corps to India, where he served with great distinction, in various engagements, and rose to the rank of Lieutenant-General. On his return from India he became M.P. for the County of Inverness.

Chieftain Macleod, a chieftain worth gowd,
Though bred amang mountains of snow,

was the poet Burns's estimate of General Macleod.
He was married to a daughter of Mackenzie of Suddy,
who died in 1784, when he was absent in India.   He
died at Guernsey in August 1801, and was succeeded
by his son, John Norman Macleod of Macleod, at one
time M.P. for Sudbury.   He contested the represent-
ation of the County of Inverness, after the Reform Act,
but was defeated by a few votes.   He died on 25th
March 1835, aged 46, and is succeeded by his son,
Norman Macleod of Macleod of Dunvegan Castle, a
Deputy Lieutenant of the County of Inverness, and
Secretary of the British Fisheries Society.   Norman
Macleod of Macleod married, in 1831, the Hon. Louisa-
Barbara, only daughter of St Andrew, 13th Lord St
John.   His son, Captain N. M. Macleod of the 74th
Highlanders, is heir apparent.

   John Macleod, young Raasay, formerly mentioned as
aiding Prince Charles in his escape, had the estate of
Raasay conveyed to him by his father, previous to his
joining the Highland army in 1745.   He was married
to a Miss Macqueen, by whom he had a numerous
family.   Dr Johnson and Boswell experienced the
generous and elegant hospitality of this family when on
their Tour.   Johnson writes :—

> Our reception exceeded our expectation. We found nothing but
> civility, elegance, and plenty. After the usual refreshments, and the
> usual conversation, the evening came upon us. The carpet was then
> rolled off the floor, the musician was called in, and the whole company
> was invited to dance ; nor did ever fairies trip it with greater alacrity.
> The general air of festivity which predominated in this place, so far
> remote from all those regions which the mind has been used to contem-
> plate as the mansions of pleasure, struck the imagination with a delight-
> ful surprise, analogous to that which is felt at an unexpected emersion
> from darkness into light.
>
> When it was time to sup, the dance ceased, and six-and-thirty persons
> sat down to two tables in the same room. After supper the ladies sung
> Erse songs, to which I listened as an English audience to an Italian
> opera, delighted with the sound of words which I did not understand.
>
> The family of Raasay consists of the laird, the lady, three sons, and
> ten daughters. More gentleness of manners, or a more pleasing appear-
> ance of domestic society, is not found in the most polished countries.

Raasay having been in London afterwards called on

Dr Johnson, who provided a magnificent and expensive entertainment in his honour.

Raasay's eldest daughter was "an elegant, well-bred woman, and celebrated for her beauty over all those regions by the name of Miss Flora Rasay." She married, in 1777, Colonel Mure Campbell, afterwards Earl of Loudon, and died soon thereafter, leaving one daughter, who became Countess of Loudon, in her own right, and was married to the Marquis of Hastings. Miss Isabella Macleod of Raasay, a sister of Miss Flora, was married to a Major Ross, who died in the East Indies, leaving one daughter, who was brought up in Raasay House, and having accompanied her cousin, the Marchioness of Hastings, to India, she married the Hon. Sir Charles Doyle. "Here she did not forget Mackay, the piper of Raasay, but had an elegant stand of pipes, of peculiar native workmanship, prepared, which she presented to him, on which occasion he composed in her honour 'Lady Doyle's Salute.'" John Macleod of Raasay was succeeded in the estates by his eldest son, James Macleod. His second son was the Rev. Malcolm Macleod, minister of Snizort, and father of the late lamented, and much venerated, Rev. Roderick Macleod of Snizort, one of the moderators of the Free Church Assembly. James Macleod rebuilt, on an extensive and elegant scale, the mansion house of Raasay. He died in 1824, and was succeeded by his son, John Macleod of Raasay, who married a daughter of Sir Donald Macleod, distinguished as a military officer in India, and son of Macleod of Bharkasaig, Skye. In 1846 Raasay's creditors sold the estate to George Rainy, Esquire, and the island is now possessed by his son, George H. Rainy, Esquire, a deputy Lieutenant of the County of Inverness, and Captain of the Skye Rifle Volunteers.

The Macleods of Rig were cadets of the family of *MacGillechallum* of Raasay. Norman Macleod of Rig had three sons, officers in the British army, during the War of Independence in America,—Captain Norman

v

Macleod, afterwards of Camustianavaig ; Captain John
Macleod, afterwards of Ollach, father of the late Dr
Archibald Macleod of North Uist, and of the late Nor-
man Macleod of Scalpay ; and Dr Murdoch Macleod,
afterwards of Kilpheder, North Uist. Two of Dr
Murdoch Macleod's sons were physicians :—Dr Murdoch
Macleod who practised in the West Indies, and died in
North Uist, and the late well-known and much esteemed
Dr Alexander Macleod, at one time Chamberlain for
Lord Macdonald, in Skye, and afterwards for Macdonald
of Clanranald, in South Uist, in which capacity he
planned and executed many beneficial improvements on
the estates of these landlords. Flora, eldest daughter
of Dr Murdoch Macleod of Kilpheder, returned from
America in the same ship with the celebrated Flora
Macdonald. She was married to the late Rev. William
Arbuckle, minister of North Uist.

CHAPTER XXV.

IT has been computed by a competent authority that
during the period of the wars with America and France,
in the latter end of the past and beginning of the
present century, the Isle of Skye produced 10,000 foot
soldiers, 600 commissioned officers under the rank of·
colonel, 48 lieutenant-colonels, 21 lieutenant-generals
and major-generals, four governors of British colonies,
one governor-general, one adjutant-general, one chief
baron of England, and one judge of the Supreme Court
of Scotland.

   Some of these officers have already been incidentally
referred to, and though it · would be interesting to
enumerate the whole, with a short sketch of the services
of each, we regret that from the want of the necessary
materials we can only mention a few of those distinguished men.

   Donald Macdonald of Castleton, whose letter to the
Lord President has been quoted, was captain of one of

the independent companies raised in Skye in 1745, and having afterwards entered the army, he rose to the rank of colonel. He was married to Isabella, daughter of William Macleod of Hamer, author of a treatise on the Second Sight, under the designation of " Theophilus Insulanus." His son, John Macdonald of Castleton, succeeded Sheriff Macleod of Ullinish as Sheriff-Substitute of Skye. He was married to Margaret, daughter of Macleod of Arnisdale, Glenelg, the grandfather of Donald Macleod, Esquire, now of Scorrybreck, better known as " Kingsburgh," he having for a long series of years maintained the characteristic hospitality of Kingsburgh House. Sheriff Macdonald died on 25th December 1826, aged eighty-seven years. Three of his sons were officers in the army ; Major Alexander Macdonald and Captain William Macdonald, who died in the East Indies, and Captain John Macdonald of the H. E. I. C. service, who died at Skirinish in 1833.

Lieutenant Allan Macdonald of Knock, who made himself so active in the Government service in 1746, was father to General Donald Macdonald, Colonel of the 55th Regiment, who was wounded in Holland in 1799.

Norman Macdonald of Scalpay, mentioned as having married a grand-daughter of " old Kingsburgh," was the father of a distinguished family. Mrs Macdonald is still remembered in Skye, not only for her accomplishments, but also for her benevolence and active interest in the promotion of religion. One of their sons was Sir John Macdonald, Adjutant-General of the British army ; another, Colonel Archibald Macdonald, held a similar appointment in India ; and a third, Colonel Alexander Macdonald, of the Horse Artillery, served with distinction at the taking of Monte Video, the Cape of Good Hope, and the Peninsular war. His conduct at the battle of Waterloo gained for him the commendation of the Duke of Wellington and Lord Hill. He became Governor of the Honduras. Another member of this family is Matthew Macdonald Hume,

Esquire, W.S., Edinburgh, father of John H. A. Macdonald, Esquire, advocate, author of a practical treatise on the criminal law of Scotland, and Lieutenant-Colonel of the " The Queen's City of Edinburgh Rifle Volunteer Brigade." The tomb of Mr and Mrs Macdonald of Scalpay in the churchyard of Kilmore, Sleat, bears the following inscription :— " In memory of Norman Macdonald, Esq. of Barnisdale, who died on the 28th December 1823, aged 81 years ; and of Susannah Macalister, his wife, who died on the 20th July 1820, aged 66 years. This tablet has been placed here by their eldest surviving son, Lieutenant-General Sir John Macdonald, K.C.B., adjutant-general of the forces, as an expression of duty and affection towards his deeply-revered and beloved parents."

The late Charles Macdonald of Ord was an officer in the army. He is celebrated by Alexander Smith in his " Summer in Skye," under the cognomen of " M'Ian," who, he writes, " entered the army at an early age ; carried colours in Ireland before the century came in ; was with Moore at Corunna ; followed Wellington through the Peninsular battles ; was with the 42d at Quatre Bras, and hurt there when the brazen cuirassiers came charging through the tall ryegrass ; and, finally, stood at Waterloo in a square that crumbled before the artillery and cavalry charges of Napoleon— crumbled but never flinched !"

In 1760 Macleod of Macleod raised a company of men on his estates in Skye, to the command of which he appointed his nephew, Captain Fothringham of Pourie. This company was embraced in " Keith's and Campbell's Highlanders," and served with distinction under Prince Ferdinand, in Germany. A good number from Macleod's estate joined the Scotch Brigade in Holland. Macleod of Talisker was a Colonel, and Macleod of Balmeanach was a Major in this brigade. " It was remarked that Colonel Macleod of Talisker, and the gentlemen of the Isle of Skye who joined the brigade in Holland, were particularly successful. They always found a ready supply of young soldiers." The hospitality of Talisker is acknowledged by Pennant, Johnson, Boswell, and Knox, in their accounts of their journeys to Skye. Professor Macleod of Aberdeen was a brother of Talisker.

Colonel Norman Macleod of Colbost was a distinguished officer, and saw much service. Three of his sons, Generals Donald and Alexander Macleod, and Sir John Macpherson Macleod, K.C.S.I., of St Kilda and Glendale, Skye, served their country with credit in India.

Norman Macleod of Bernisdale, afterwards of Peninduin, married to Ann, daughter of Norman Macleod of Bernera, was a captain in the army. He died in 1804. His eldest son, Donald Macleod, was Inspector General of Hospitals in Bengal, and died in 1840. His second son, Roderick Macleod, was killed at the siege of St Sebastian. William Macleod of Orbost was his third son.

Captain Cyprus Macleod of Stein, Captain Alexander Macleod of Vatten, Captain Kenneth Macaskill of Rhundunan, Captain —— Maccrimmon from Durinish, afterwards of Cape Coast Castle, were all brave soldiers of that period. Major-General Sir John Macaskill, son of Dr Macaskill of Bracadale, was also a distinguished officer, and served his country with honour in India.

In the year 1803 two regiments of volunteers were formed in Skye. The 1st regiment, numbering 507 men, was commanded by Lieutenant-Colonel James Macleod of Raasay. The second regiment, numbering 510, was commanded by Lieutenant-Colonel A. Macdonald of Lynedale. On 16th November 1803, a meeting of the officers of the volunteers was held at Portree, at which Lieutenant-Colonel Macleod of Raasay, Lieutenant-Colonel Macdonald of Lynedale, Major Alexander Macdonald of Mugstot, Major John Campbell of Kingsburgh, Norman Macdonald of Scalpay, and Lachlan Mackinnon of Corry, were present. It was then resolved that Sconser should be the place of general rendezvous for the southern battalion, and Portree for the northern battalion, where they were to assemble " upon the first intelligence of the landing of an enemy." Twenty alarm posts were fixed upon, which were to be supplied with " proper combustible fit for making signals by day and night."

A regiment of local militia, of 500 men, was formed in Skye in 1811.

Several of the ministers of Skye, in the last century, were highly educated and talented men. The Rev. John Macpherson, D. D., minister of the Parish of Sleat, was distinguished for his learning and talents. He composed several pieces of Latin poetry. Of one of these Dr Johnson said, " It does him honour, he has a great deal of Latin, and good Latin." Dr Macpherson was author of " Critical Dissertations on the Origin, Antiquities, Language, Government, Manners, and Religion of the ancient Caledonians, their Posterity the Picts, and the British and Irish Scots." This work was published in 1768 (after the Doctor's death), by his son, Sir John Macpherson, at one time Governor-General of Bengal, who wrote a preface to the book, in which he has the following remarks upon his father :—" Excluded by the peculiar situation of the place of his residence from the society of the learned, he indulged his singular passion for literature among a few good books. Though the natural bent of his genius turned towards the belles-lettres, he sometimes amused himself in disquisitions of a more serious nature. Being master of the Celtic, in all its branches, he took pleasure in tracing other languages to that general source of all the ancient and modern tongues of Europe." The Doctor was succeeded in the Parish of Sleat by his son, the Rev. Martin Macpherson, " a man of intelligence and taste," who died in 1812.

The Rev. Donald Macqueen, minister of the Parish of Kilmuir, was also an eminent man. He supported the evangelical party in the Church of Scotland, and is mentioned with honour by his contemporary, Dr John

Erskine, in his "Sketches of Church History." Dr Macqueen was author of a "Dissertation on the Government of the People in the Western Isles," published with Pennant's Tour, and of "Letters on Hume's History." He was employed by the General Assembly of the Church of Scotland, with other learned ministers, to revise the translation of the Five Books of Moses (the Pentateuch), "and in the course of performing this task, Dr Macqueen wrote very learned and interesting remarks on the customs of primitive nations, contained in a series of letters to Mr Stewart of Luss, well worthy of being communicated to the Republic of Letters." He was admitted a corresponding member of the Society of Antiquaries on 13th February 1781, and some of his writings are published in the transactions of that society. The following notices of him are gleaned from Boswell's Tour :—

In a little while arrived Mr Donald Macqueen himself, a decent minister, an elderly man, with his own black hair, courteous, and rather slow of speech, but candid, sensible, and well informed—nay learned. . . . He (Dr Johnson) was pleased with Macqueen, and said to me, "This is a critical man, Sir, there must be great vigour of mind to make him cultivate learning so much, in the Isle of Skye, where he might do without it ; it is wonderful how many of the new publications he has ; there must be a snatch of every opportunity." Mr Macqueen told me that his brother (who is the fourth generation of the family, following each other as ministers of the parish of Snizort) and he joined together, and bought from time to time such books as had reputation.

Dr Macqueen died at Raasay in 1785. One of his sons was parish minister of Applecross, another was a physician in Norwich, and a daughter was married to the Rev. Roderick Macleod, parish minister of Bracadale, successor to the Rev. William Macleod (brother of Sheriff Macleod, Ullinish), and predecessor to the Rev. John Shaw, whose labours were much blessed and appreciated in that parish.

The Rev. John Nicolson was parish minister of Portree for upwards of forty years. He died in 1803, bequeathing the sum of £140 as a fund for behoof of the poor of the parish of Portree. He is described in the "Old Statistical Account" as "a man of primitive

manners and exemplary conduct, of a sincere, bene-
volent, and charitable disposition, of untainted
rectitude and uprightness." It is related that on one
occasion, when Lord Macdonald was hearing Mr Nicolson preach at Portree, he enquired of Mr Nicolson, after
the service, how it was he omitted to pray for him
specially, he being present, and it being customary on
such occasions to mention the proprietor in the prayers.
Mr Nicolson replied, " I included you in the great bulk
of sinners." Mr Nicolson was succeeded as parish
minister by the parochial teacher, the Rev. Alexander
Campbell, son of Mr Campbell of Cornlarach, near
Dunvegan, and brother of the Rev. Donald Campbell,
D.D., of Kilninver and Kilmelfort. Mr Campbell was
succeeded by the late Rev. Coll Macdonald.

It is related that the state of evangelical religion in
Skye was at a low ebb about the close of the last
century, but that much good resulted from a visit to
the island about the year 1800, of the Rev. Mr
Farquharson, a dissenting minister. While Mr
Farquharson was preaching in the open air at Earlish,
from the words in Rev. iii. & 20, " Behold I stand at
the door and knock ; if any man hear my voice and
open the door, I will come into him, and will sup with
him, and he with me," blind Donald Munro, then a
violinist, was converted. Though blind from his boy-
hood, he was both intelligent and talented. He became
a lay preacher, holding forth in a meeting house built
for him in Snizort, and was eminently blessed in being
the means of bringing many to the knowledge of the
truth. He repeated the Psalms and Scriptures correctly
from memory, giving chapter and verse. He kept
himself well informed as to the public events of the
day ; and his eminent piety and sound wisdom caused
many to resort to him for advice, both in their spiritual
and temporal affairs.

The establishment of the schools of the Gaelic School
Society in Skye in 1811 proved a great blessing, as
they brought within the reach of many the knowledge

of the Scriptures in their own language, which they would otherwise have been ignorant of. These schools were taught by a superior class of men, men of approved piety and discretion, who, by their teaching and example, materially contributed to the religious character of the island.

Without touching on the events which have transpired in Skye within the past sixty years, I must now conclude these imperfect sketches. I am sensible that much that would be interesting has been omitted, and that probably errors have been committed in part of what is written, though I have endeavoured to avoid such. I only hope that the perusal of the foregoing pages may afford as much pleasure to the reader, as the compiling of them, and the tracing of the history and traditions of his native isle, has afforded the writer. To the sons of Skye, all that pertains to the history of their native isle cannot fail to be interesting, for whether dwelling under the shadow of its mountain peaks, or pushing their fortunes in a foreign land, their patriotic spirit is such as might lead them to exclaim—

> Loved Isle of Skye! "what mortal hand
> Can e'er untie the filial band
> That knits me to thy rugged strand?"

CPSIA information can be obtained
at www.ICGtesting.com
Printed in the USA
BVHW07s1038111018
529884BV00014B/434/P